D1433548

Please renew/return this item by the last date shown.

So that your telephone call is charged at local rate, please call the numbers as set out below:

	From Area codes 01923 or 0208:	From the rest of Herts:
Renewals:	01923 471373	01438 737373
Enquiries:	01923 471333	01438 737333
Minicom:	01923 471599	01438 737599

L32b

DICK WHITTINGTON
FACT AND FABLE

By the same Author:

HUMOUR (SHORT STORIES)
A Roof over my Head
The Sky over my Head

PHILATELY
Ascension—The Stamps and Postal History

DICK WHITTINGTON
FACT AND FABLE

by

John Attwood

Regency Press (London & New York) Ltd.
125 High Holborn, London WC1V 6QA

Copyright © 1988 by John Attwood

This book is copyrighted under the Berne Convention.
No portion may be reproduced by any process without
the copyright holder's written permission except for the
purposes of reviewing or criticism, as permitted under
the Copyright Act of 1956.

HERTFORDSHIRE
COUNTY LIBRARY

B|WH| | 942.03'7'0924|wHI

ISBN 0 7212 0739 1

Printed and bound in Great Britain by
Buckland Press Ltd., Dover, Kent.

To my wife Barbara

My heartfelt thanks for unwittingly giving me the exciting idea of writing this book and for the ongoing help so readily given.

CONTENTS

PART 1

LIST OF ILLUSTRATIONS

ACKNOWLEDGEMENTS

Plate 4: Coberley Court and St. Giles Church—*The Rev. Canon S. I. Pulford, The Rectory, Coberley, Cheltenham, Glos.*

Plate 7: Church of St. John the Evangelist, Pauntley—*Mrs. J. Elgood, Hon. Sec., Pauntley P.C.C.*

Plate 11: Embroidered cushion of Dick Whittington and his Cat—*The Dean and Chapter of Gloucester Cathedral.*

Plate 18: Dick Whittington window—*Miss P. Hall, Verger, Church of St. Michael Paternoster Royal.*

ACKNOWLEDGEMENTS

First, and foremost, I am indebted to Sir Greville Spratt, the present Lord Mayor of London, for taking the time to read, and contribute such a very generous FOREWORD to my book.

For information, so helpful in the research stage, I would express my thanks to the following:—

Mrs. Cynthia Camidge for being such an able, and willing, research assistant. Mrs. Joan Dacre, Voluntary Services Co-ordinator, for historical data regarding "The Hospital on the Hill". Mr. John Deuchar, Tutor, Whittington College, Felbridge for information on the College and for editing my draft text. Guildhall Public Relations office and Guildhall staff for permission to photograph in the "Old" library and for providing much relevant, and lesser known, information on the Guildhall. Miss P. Hall, Verger, Church of St. Michael Paternoster Royal, for the details of the cat found in Dick Whittington's tomb and for permission to reproduce the photograph of the cat. Mr. Glyn Jones, Bridge Clerk to the Rochester Bridge Trust for the reference to Dick Whittington in the Trust archives. Mr. Dennis Martin, Director, Players' Theatre, regarding the 1985 performance of *Whittington Junior and His Sensation Cat*. Miss Anne Sutton, Archivist to the Mercers' Company for background information on Dick Whittington and for providing such an extensive, and useful, bibliography relevant to the history of Medieval London. Mrs. Pamela Waring for providing a copy of the Pedigree of the family of Whittington by the Rev. Samuel Lysons.

For permission to quote extracts for the following publications:—

Basil Blakwell, publishers, *They saw It Happen, 55BC-1485*. Athlone Press Ltd., publishers, *The Charity of Richard Whittington*. Oxford University Press, publishers, *Dictionary of National Biography, vol. xxi*.

FOREWORD
by The Right Honourable The Lord Mayor
Sir Greville Spratt, GBE, TD, DL, DLitt

1989 sees the 800th anniversary of the foundation of London's Mayoralty, and one of the most famous holders of that ancient office was the Mercer, Richard Whittington, whose four terms of office spanned the reigns of three Kings.

There is a Whittington of romance and a Whittington of reality, and in this particularly well researched and documented new study of London's best known citizen, the writer John Attwood has separated fact from fable with admirable skill and clarity.

He has written a book that gives a rewarding insight into a remarkable man, and provides an absorbing account of civic duty and responsibility.

Dr. Johnson once said that a man will turn over half a library to make one book. The author of this fascinating study has done just that in producing a work which I commend to all lovers of London and its long history.

Greville Spratt.

Lord Mayor

PART 1

DICK WHITTINGTON
THE FACTS

INTRODUCTION

To fully appreciate the considerable achievements of Richard Whittington as Merchant, Legislator, Financier and Public Benefactor, I believe that it is necessary to review the chaotic state of England immediately before he was born in 1357 and during those formative years leading to manhood.

From 1348 to 1351 there was a major outbreak of bubonic plague which became known as the Black Death. The main outbreak was followed by three lesser outbreaks in 1356, 1361-62 and 1368-69.[1] By 1350 about half the population of England had died and although the hardest hit were the townspeople who were living in cramped and unhygienic conditions, the villagers were far from immune from this fatal affliction.[2]

In Medieval England the teachers were the priests and the friars, so when half the monks at Westminster Abbey, including the abbot, and forty-seven of the sixty monks at St. Albans, had died,[2] one can appreciate the devastating affect this was going to have on the education and learning of the coming generations. Thomas Bradwardine, who had been newly ordained Archbishop of Canterbury, only survived two days in London.[1]

Numerous parish churches throughout the country, which had been planned, remained uncompleted because there were just no masons available for the building work. There was also a shortage of labour and master craftsmen, not only masons. Also many masters were short of apprentices and merchants were without servants. In the villages corn was left uncut and women had to help with the ploughing. In many cases the smaller villages had to be abandoned.[2]

Before the Black Death labour had been cheap and land scarce, but now the situation was reversed. Land owners found that their villeins, or serfs, disappeared overnight and were hidden by friends, since if they could hide successfully for a year and a day they became legally free and in the circumstances then prevailing could find a ready market, at good wages, for their labour.[2]

By 1381 the church had become inefficient and was giving no guidance or making any serious attempt to educate the people. So without proper leadership and the failure of the French wars, which had been going on since 1338, England was overrun by unemployed soldiers, men without land or property and fugitive serfs.[2] All such unrest was to be the catalyst for future uprisings throughout the country.

The French wars having lasted on and off for over a hundred years had left the country greatly in debt and with only the towns of Calais, Bordeaux and Bayonne left in English hands. This shortage of much needed funds resulted in the imposition of very high and, in many cases, punitive taxes which, in turn, touched off a social revolution throughout the country.[2]

Wat Tyler, variously described as an old soldier,[2] a tiler of houses, a bad man and an enemy of the nobility,[4] turned out the Kentish men in protest against the Poll Tax which he, and his followers, considered to be grossly unfair[2]. The men of Essex, Sussex, Bedford and the adjoining counties joined the men of Kent and marched on London.[4] This uprising, in its initial stages, was intended as an orderly protest. However, when the protestors, about sixty thousand in all, reached the gates of the City of London the discontented workers in the City opened the[2] six gates[3] in the City wall and allowed the marchers in. It was the stabbing to death of Wat Tyler by William Walworth, the then Mayor of London, which turned an orderly protest into a murderous riot. The mob opened the prisons and broke into the Tower of London, murdered the Treasurer and the Archbishop of Canterbury and generally looted and burnt indiscriminately.[2]

The actual dagger which is believed to have been used to kill Wat Tyler is today one of the prized possessions of the Fishmongers' Company.[3] The Sword of St. Paul in the arms of the City of London came to be misinterpreted as that dagger.[4] Also in the Fishmongers' Hall is a life-sized wooden statue of Sir William Walworth carved by Peirce in 1684.[5]

By now the situation in the City of London was out of hand and fearing a general massacre, Richard II took over the leadership of the peasant army and led them out of the City.[2] Considering that the King was only fourteen years old and had only been on the throne for four years, this action showed a high degree of courage and diplomacy.

It is not surprising that there exists another version of events leading up to the killing of Wat Tyler which was much less flattering to the King. In this other account Wat Tyler's men of Kent and those from Essex were let into the City on the thirteenth of June 1381 and burnt to the ground the mansion of Sir John, Duke of Lancaster, together with all the houses in the immediate vicinity of the Church of the Hospital of St. John of Jerusalem, without Smethefield. On the following day, the King met the rebels at "Mileende", having ridden out from the Tower of London with his retinue, and agreed that they, the rebels, could find and kill all those in the City who were the King's enemies.[4]

On the fifteenth of June at Smethefield, where the King and his retinue were facing the bloodthirsty mob, the Mayor, William Walworth, killed their leader, Wat Tyler, and went, unhurt, with the King to a field in the place now known as Clerkenwell. The mob, not satisfied, wanted the King to give them the head of the Mayor but William Walworth had, at the King's request, returned to the City, raised a large citizen army loyal to the King, and then returned to surround the leaderless mob. The King allowed the mob to disperse and returning to the City, Richard II knighted William Walworth, Nicholas Brembre, John Phelipot and Robert Launde.[4]

So it was against this background that Dick Whittington came to London to be apprenticed and acquire through hard work and ability great wealth and stature in the City by his twenty-first birthday.

John Attwood.

SOURCE REFERENCES
1. Life in Medieval England.
2. History of England.
3. In Search of London.
4. They Saw It Happen, 55 B.C.-1485.
5. A Short History of Fishmongers' Hall.

THE WHITTINGTON FAMILY

Samuel Lysons in his "Pedigree of the family of Whittington" asserts that Sir William Whittington, Dick Whittington's father, married Joan, daughter of William Mansel, and that they had at least three sons. Also that Lady Joan married Thomas Berkeley of Coberley after Sir William's death. Furthermore Samuel Lysons writes that Sir William was outlawed just before his death and that Joan, his wife, had remarried. No reason is advanced for Sir William having had to suffer the heavy punishment of being made an outlaw.[1]

In the church pamphlet of St. John the Evangelist, Pauntley, can be found the following which is presented as fact. Sir William Whittington married Sir Thomas Berkeley's widow in 1352 and was subsequently outlawed for marrying a Berkeley widow without Royal sanction. Sir William remained an outlaw until his death on the seventeenth of March 1358. Dick Whittington was the son of Sir William and Dame Joan according to the Whittington College records which were authenticated by Dick Whittington himself. Dame Joan being the daughter of William Mansel is only classed as a probability rather than as a fact. Finally this same church pamphlet states that Dick Whittington had an older brother, William, born in 1335 and possibly by a different mother.[7]

The church pamphlet of Saint Giles, Coberley, indicates that Sir Thomas Berkeley died about 1350 and that his wife, Lady Joan, married her second husband, Sir William Whittington, who died an outlaw a few years after their son, Dick Whittington, was born.[1]

A study of the aforementioned historical data presents several anomalies. The major difficulty is that Samuel Lysons has Lady Joan's first husband as Sir William Whittington, followed by a second marriage to Thomas Berkeley whereas the two church pamphlets infer a reversal in the order of these two marriages. Also if Lady Joan was married to Thomas Berkeley after Sir William's death, then there would be no reason for him being outlawed on the grounds of not having obtained a Royal sanction.

From other sources, and not only the pamphlet in the Church of Saint Giles, it can be reasonably inferred that Dick Whittington was born after 1355, most probably in 1357. So we have William, the eldest son, born in 1335; Dick Whittington, the youngest son, born in 1357; Sir Thomas Berkeley dying in about 1350 and Sir William Whittington dying in 1358. Add to the foregoing the accepted concept that Lady Joan was at one time or the other, the wife of both men the end result makes no logical sense. Unfortunately the lack of parish registers in these critical years compounds the problem.

A hint to a possibly correct solution might be found in the St. John the Evangelist pamphlet where it suggests that the eldest son, William, and Dick Whittington had different mothers.[7] Put another way this could infer that Joan Mansel and Lady Joan, Sir Thomas's widow, were two different people and both, by chance, having the same christian name has led to confusion.

So if we follow through with such a proposition we have Sir William Whittington marrying Joan Mansel, possibly about 1330, and they having two sons, William and Robert. Lady Joan, born Mansel, dies about 1350 and Sir William Whittington marries, in 1352, the widow of Sir Thomas Berkeley, who happens, by coincidence, to have the christian name of Joan. Sir William becomes an outlaw for marrying Lady Joan Berkeley without the King's consent and a year before he dies Dick Whittington is born.

Although Dick Whittington was not born at Coberley, it is said that he spent much of his childhood at Coberley Hall. This makes good sense, since if the above proposed family line of descent is accepted Dick Whittington's mother was formerly a Berkeley. It would seem natural, therefore, that, after a bare six years of marriage to a disgraced and outlawed husband, Lady Joan would wish to spend more time at Coberley than at Pauntley.

It has been said that Dick Whittington was not treated with a great deal of kindness and affection by his two older brothers. This again would be very understandable if we accept the thesis that William and Robert had a different mother from Dick Whittington.

The South Chapel of Coberley church was endowed and built by Sir Thomas Berkeley in about 1340 and dedicated to the Virgin Mary. In the South Chapel can now be found the effigies of Sir Thomas Berkeley and his wife, Lady Joan, these freestone effigies having been removed from the Sanctuary to their present position in 1870.[6] Again, accepting that the widowed Lady Joan was married for only six years to a disgraced husband, it would seem quite logical that she would wish to be buried at Coberley rather than at Pauntley.

On the south boundary of the churchyard of the Church of Saint Giles, there exists today a high wall which was part of the enclosure of the original manor house.[6]

So it was that, at the appropriate age, Dick Whittington left Gloucestershire and came to the City of London to be apprenticed to a mercer and, in due time, marry Alice, the daughter of Sir Ivo FitzWaryn.[3] Sir Ivo FitzWaryn died in September 1414 and Alice, having predeceased her father, did not therefore inherit any of her father's estates which were considerable and comprised property in the south-west counties, principally Dorset and Devon. The FitzWaryn estates passed to Alice's sister, Alianor, and not, therefore, by marriage into the Whittington family.[3] When Dick Whittington came to London he was not the poor orphan boy of the fable but neither was he wealthy[7] as being the youngest son, he did not inherit the family estates and Pauntley was only assessed at the time at about a knight's fee of about twenty pounds per annum.[7]

Inquisitions made on Sir Ivo FitzWaryn's death show his daughter, Alice, and Dick Whittington as having been parties to deeds by which Sir Ivo FitzWaryn had granted them both, on his death, the reversion of certain manors in Somerset and land in Wiltshire. Possibly this inheritance was intended as a dowry but since Alice had died some five years before her[3] father it is not at all clear who was the ultimate beneficiary, Dick Whittington or Alice's sister, Alianor.

Sir Ivo FitzWaryn's Will was proved on the fifth of February 1415 and to Dick Whittington, his executor, he bequeathed, "a silver gilt cup with cover and a pair of pure gold rosaries, enamelled in red with jewels of gold enamelled with white in the form of the head of St. John the Baptist".[5]

PAUNTLEY ESTATE

For his support in the Norman Conquest, Walter de Laci, one of William the Conqueror's leading soldiers, was granted some one hundred and twenty manors including that of Pauntley and the

Coberley Court and St. Giles Church.

Effigies of Sir Thomas Berkeley and Lady Joan.

adjoining area, then called "Ledene". Walter de Laci's niece married Ansfrid of Cormeilles who thereby came into possession of Pauntley which was part of her dowry.

Walter de Cormeilles or de Pauntley is believed to have built Pauntley Church, now called St. John the Evangelist, in about 1170. Walter de Pauntley was the grandson or great grandson of Ansfrid and this possible benefaction makes logical sense since the Benedictine Abbey of Cormeilles in Normandy was granted "the impropriation and advowson (profits and right of appointment of the priest) appertaining to the newly built little chapel at Pauntley".[7] Walter de Pauntley died in 1248 and the estates passed to his daughter, the Pauntley heiress, Margaret. By her first marriage to John de Solers the estate was conveyed into the Solers family of Hope Solers, Herefordshire (present day name is Sollers Hope).[1]

The Pauntley estate remained with the Solers family until the death, in 1276, of John de Solers' son (same name) when it passed to his son-in-law, William Whittington, eldest son of William Whittington of Upton, Warwickshire and Maud Solers, John de Solers' daughter. In 1332 the manor, Pauntley Court, and the estate were inherited by Sir William Whittington, Dick Whittington's father.[7]

When Sir William Whittington died in outlawry the estate passed to Dick Whittington's brother, William, and on the latter's death to the next eldest brother, Robert. On the twelfth of March 1358, five days before Sir William Whittington's death, Pauntley, as a result of his outlawry, was handed over to the Crown on a suit brought by William de Southam for debt. The debt presumably having been settled, the Pauntley estate continued in Whittington ownership until 1546 when it was divided amongst the six daughters of Thomas Whittington whose burial is recorded in the earliest parish register of Pauntley. One of the daughters, Elizabeth by name, had died in 1543 and her share, the manor of Pauntley was conveyed to her husband, Sir Giles Pole of Sapperton.[7]

Pauntley Court and the church are situated about nine miles from Gloucester beside the river Leadon and on the borders of Herefordshire and Worcestershire[1] just north of the Forest of Dean.

In 1660, on the restoration of the Monarchy, the last male heir of the Pole family sold the manor to Henry Somerset of the family of the Duke of Beaufort and through various heiresses the Duke of Beaufort retained an interest in Pauntley Court until 1773.[7]

The existing Pauntley Court is privately owned and only some two hundred years old. However, a half-timbered wing, which had in the past served as a granary, may have been built by the Whittington's around 1500.[7] According to Samuel Lysons, "the Manor of Pauntley was only worth about twenty pounds in about 1860 and the parish was mainly moorland and chase which had hardly improved in value since the Norman Conquest". Lysons further described Pauntley, "as being remote but pleasing and picturesque".[1]

It is said that the population of Pauntley in about 1881 was only two hundred and fifty-six and was considered to be even less in Dick Whittington's time.[2] The population in 1700 was one hundred and fifteen, in 1770 it was eighty-seven and in 1801 it was two hundred and fifteen with forty-one inhabited houses. A more recent census in 1971 put the population at only one hundred and thirty-five.[7]

PAUNTLEY CHURCH

As has already been said, the Pauntley Church of St. John the Evangelist dates from about 1170. In recent years the Mercers' Company has helped with the on-going restoration work and in particular the repointing of the tower. The North Sanctuary window bearing the Whittington Arms has been inaccurately repaired with clear glass instead of red in the top pane.[7]

On the south wall is a brass memorial plate to Elizabeth Pole, one of the six daughters of Thomas Whittington, which bears the following inscription:—

"Here lieth Elizabeth late wife of Sir Giles Pole Knight one
of the daughters and sixth coheiress - of Thomas
Whittington Esquire deceased which Elizabeth passed from
this transitory life the fourth day of September in the year
of our Lord God 1543 on whose soul God have mercy."

Also beneath the altar table is a ledger stone inscribed, "CHARLES HENRY WHITTINGTON, 1872-1961, father of the present Richard Whittington". There is also little doubt that Dick Whittington was baptised in this church and born in the nearby manor house.

As a direct result of such a close association, the Lord Mayor of London, the Mayor of Gloucester, representatives of the Mercers' Company and local authorities together with members of the Whittington family, all came to the church in 1959 to celebrate the six hundredth anniversary of Dick Whittington's birth. The City of London

Pauntley Court.

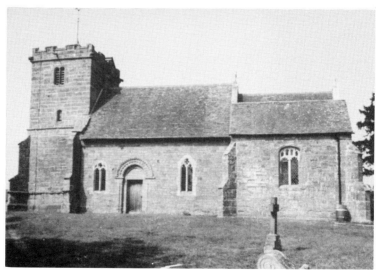

Church of St. John the Evangelist, Pauntley.

presented to the church a silver alms dish, which is now on display in the Gloucester Cathedral Treasury. There is also a commemorative plaque at Pauntley Court.[7]

WHITTINGTON COAT OF ARMS
The Coat of Arms of the Whittington family has been described by Lysons in the following terms:—
"Gules, a Fesse componé or (checky), Or and Azure.
Crest—a lion's head, erased Sable, Langued Gules."[1]
Dick Whittington changed the family crest from a lion's head to a bee, or mayfly, with the wings tipped with gold. It is surmised that he was attempting to "symbolise the slow and patient toil from which success is obtained".[2]

It has been stated that in 1407 Dick Whittington received a knighthood from Henry V and entertained the King and Queen at Guildhall. However there seems to be no evidence to substantiate this assertion by Samuel Lysons.[1] In fact national policy in the thirteenth century was to award knighthoods to landowners with incomes above a specific level so that they could be obliged to organise national defence and do the work of local government. This was not popular and many preferred to pay a fine of up to twenty pounds to be excused the honour. The income level was raised once during the reign of Edward II to fifty pounds and thereafter fixed at forty pounds on income from rents, but merchants who had forty pounds from rents were just as reluctant as the landowners to accept a knighthood. This refusal so angered Richard II that in 1392 he suspended the City's liberties and two years later extracted ten thousand pounds from the citizens for their restoration. There were no merchant knights in the City of London in 1412, nor in 1436,[4] so it can be reasonably held to be quite incorrect to refer to Dick Whittington as Sir Richard.

SOURCE REFERENCES
1. The Model Merchant of the Middle Ages.
2. Sir Richard Whittington.
3 History of Dorset.
4. The Merchant Class of Medieval London.
5. Register of Henry Chichele.
6. The Church of Saint Giles, Coberley—church pamphlet.
7. St. John the Evangelist, Pauntley—church pamphlet.

WILLIAM DE WHITYNTON=
in coun. Warwick,
non longe ab Haslar.

WILLIAM DE WHITYNTON=HARISSA, or HAWISE, sister and
coheir of Hugh Aguillon,
of Upton, Co. Warwick.
Inq. p. m., Edw. I.

RICHARD DE WHITYNGTON,
manucaptor of John Monywood,
Citizen, returned for Hereford,
4 Ed. II., 1311. *Parliamentary
Writs.*

Pedigree
of the family of
Whittington
of
Pauntley, Notgrove, Lye,
Rodborough, Rodmarton, Tainton, Stroud,
Lippiatt, and
Cold Ashton, in the County of Gloucester.
Collected from
Pedigrees in the British Museum, Heralds' College,
and other sources,
By the Rev. Samuel Lysons, M.A.

WILLIAM DE WHITYNGTON=CATHERINE,		Another	ROBERT WHITY
died seized of Pauntley, 22 Rich.	sister and heir of	son,	High sheriff of Glouceste
II., A.D. 1399, held the Manor	John de Staunton.	Guy.	3 Henry IV., A.D. 140
under Roger Mortimer, Earl of	Addl. MSS. Brit.	*Inquis. p. m.,*	8 Henry IV., A.D. 1407
March, ob. a. p., and was suc-	Mus. 5529 Pluto.	19 Henry VI.	to his brother in the Est
ceeded by his brother Robert.			Pauntley, Solers Hope
See *Cal. Inquis. post mort.,*			Staunton. Will Prov
22 Rich. II., vol, 3, p. 235.			13th of Feb. 1424

WALTER DE PAUNTLEY

Second Marriage   *First Marriage*
RICHARD DE SUTTON=MARGARET DE PAUNTLEY=JOHN DE SOLERS, of Solers Hope,
sole heir.   Co. Hereford

WALTER DE SOLERS   **THOMAS DE SOLERS**

JOHN DE SOLERS
ob. 4 Edwd. 1st, A.D. 1276.

WILLIAM DE WHITYNTON=MAUD, daughter and heir
of Pauntley, died   of John de Solers, of Solers
12 Edw. I., A.D. 1284.   Hope, Co. Hereford.
Possessed the Manor of
Pauntley, according to
the Sheriffs' Returns in 1281.

Sir WILLIAM DE WHITYNGTON=JOAN, daughter and heir of Robert Linet,
Levied a line of the Manor of Pauntley   or Roger de Lynot, remarried, after
to himself for life, remainder to his son   her husband's death, to Reginald de
William, and Joan, his son's wife, ob.   Abbenhall, who was living 1336-7.
5 Edw. III., A.D. 1332.
See Sir Robert Atkyns' *History of*
Gloucestershire, certified as Lord of
Pauntley, Gloucestershire, and Solers
Hope, Hereford, 9 Ed. II., 1316.

Sir WILLIAM DE WHITYNGDON=JOAN, daughter of William Mansel, who was High Sheriff
died seized of Pauntley and Solers   of Co. Glor. 1308. Remarried after her husband's
Hope, Co. Hereford, 33 Edw. III.,   decease to Thomas Berkeley, of Coberley, Co. Glor.,
A.D. 1360. *Outlawed, utkgatus.*   who was High Sheriff of Glor. in 1333 and 1334.
Cal. Inquis. post mort., 33 Ed. III.,   See Sir Robert Atkyns' *History of Gloucestershire,* under
Vol. 2, No. 93, named as his father   *Pauntley and Stoke Orchard,* in Cleeve Parish.
by Sir Richard Whittington.   See also *Cal. Inquis. post mort.,* Vol. 2, p. 323, and Vol. 4, p 454,
   46 and 47 Edw. III., A.D. 1373-4, named as his mother
   by Sir Richard Whittington.

MARGERY, daughter   **SIR RICHARD WHITYNGTON=ALICE**, daughter of Sir Hugh, or Ivo Fitz-
of ——Porcaford,   born about 1360; Alderman of London   warren, and Molde, or Matilda, his wife.
executrix of her   and Sheriff, A.D. 1393; Mayor, 1397,   See Whityngton's Will, Hustings Court,
husband's will.   1406-7, and 1419; M.P. for London,   London and the *Ordinances\ of his*
   1416; ob. a. p., 1423.   *College*, at Mercers' Hall, London.

THE MERCHANT

It was a popular belief that Dick Whittington was apprenticed to his future father-in-law, Sir Ivo FitzWaryn, to learn the trade of mercer in the City of London.[1] This would have been, if true, about 1370 when he was thirteen years old. Unfortunately the Mercers' Company records are not complete for the late fourteenth and early fifteenth centuries. Such gaps in the Company's records together with the fact that in about 1371 the Mercers' Company was late in obtaining Letters Patent and therefore, initially, an unauthorised Guild,[1] have done nothing to prove, or disprove, the original belief of Sir Ivo FitzWaryn as Master and Dick Whittington his apprentice.

There is no doubt that Dick Whittington was apprenticed to learn the mercer's trade and for which he would have been obliged to pay two shillings and sixpence on entry and three shillings and fourpence on closure, normally seven years later.[1] At some date before 1457 the Mercers' Company made a ten-year term of apprenticeship compulsory and by 1501 were refusing to enrol any apprentice under the age of sixteen.

Only sons of City freemen, or those from honourable families were admitted to apprenticeship.[1] By 1404 the Mercers' Company had agreed that no apprentice would be admitted until the craft master had confirmed that he was "a free man born and freeman's son". Any previous connection with an unsavoury occupation could be grounds for disqualifying a potential apprentice and, for example, country pedlars were refused entry since they were generally believed to handle stolen goods.[9]

From the beginning the City Livery Companies took great care to see that individual members behaved correctly both as regards their business dealings and their treatment of apprentices. In the case of the Mercers' Company there were four Wardenships which, between 1390 and 1460, were held by one hundred and fifty-eight different men.[6] The Warden's duties included the checking of the premises and goods of their members and also seeing that the terms of indenture of apprentices were being followed. Any master who did not properly house, feed, clothe and teach his apprentices could have them taken away and indentured to a new master.[2]

The elected Wardens together with the Master wielded considerable power and authority and the Mercers' Court, on its own authority, forbade members to transport goods to other towns for sale or peddle in the countryside. One member was fined ten pounds but this was reduced to one pound on the condition that he "swore on the book" not to do it again.[9] Another was sent to prison for failure to observe a boycott that had been imposed on a fellow member for breach of a price agreement.[6] After election, every Warden of a City Company had to take an oath before the Mayor and Aldermen that he would be loyal to the City and the King, be honest and impartial and would administer all the approved Company craft ordinances and none other. A City Ordinance of 1364 laid down penalties for Wardens who were found to be "rebellious, contrary and disturbing", ranging from a ten shilling fine and ten days in prison for the first offence to a forty shilling fine and forty days in prison for the fourth offence.[10]

Dick Whittington held the office of Master of the Mercers' Company three times, in 1395/6, 1401/2 and 1408/9.[7]

A citizen, or freeman, of London was a person who had sworn his loyalty to the City government and had agreed to take his share of taxation and public duty.[6] In addition the aspiring citizen had to provide evidence that he had a good reputation and was capable of earning a living at his chosen trade. If he had been apprenticed to a citizen, his master's sponsorship was sufficient but if he was seeking to become a citizen by redemption, that is, by purchase, he was supposed to find six citizen assurities.[10] The redemption fee was raised in 1364 to sixty shillings. They alone could exercise local political rights, buy and resell goods and keep retail shops.[10] London custom also allowed every citizen to buy and sell wholesale whatever commodities he pleased and situations existed of a surgeon trading in wool and a barber buying fur from a skinner.[6]

It was against this background that in about 1379 Dick Whittington opened a shop in London and assisted by five apprentices,[3] he provided, over the next twenty-seven years, velvets, damasks and other luxury mercery to the wealthy, the nobility and to Henry IV.[4] Thomas Roos was apprenticed to Dick Whittington in 1392 and Henry London in 1401.[8]

In 1389 Dick Whittington sold his first two cloths of gold to the King. This was followed in 1392-4 by the sale of further valuable mercery, including cloth of gold, to the Court of Richard II, known as the "Great Wardrobe", for which Dick Whittington received at least three thousand pounds.[12] Also in 1401 and 1406 Dick Whittington provided the wedding dresses for the two daughters of Henry IV. Princess Blanche's wedding dress cost £215.13s.4d. and that of Princess Phillipa £248.10s.6d.[1] Regarding Dick Whittington's apprentices it should be mentioned that mercers, who were in business, had to rely to a very considerable extent on apprentice labour. Since such persons were employed primarily as sales assistants rather than as trainee mercers, the Mercers' Company allowed them to enrol at the younger age of twelve but required them to be indentured for a period of fourteen years.[11]

Calendars and Inventories of the Exchequer proved that Dick Whittington dealt in wool and costly dresses made from wool and other materials for both nobility and royalty.[3] It is suspected that Dick Whittington's success and entry into the profitable mercer's trade at such a comparatively young age was due more to the influence of aristocratic friends rather than the result of having initially any substantial financial capital.[6]

Dick Whittington was assisted in the success of his chosen trade by the fact that foreign merchants could only sell to the City on a wholesale basis. This resulted in the London merchants being able to fix their own prices at such a very low level as to drive the foreign custom away.[1]

A "foreign" merchant was one who was unenfranchised, that is one who, for one reason or another, had not achieved the status of citizen or freeman, but nevertheless was English-born or born in London. Those who had been born overseas and were not naturalised were termed "aliens".[6]

Since reference has been made to the term "livery", some words of explanation would seem to be in order. By the fifteenth century the Merchant Companies, such as the Mercers, had divided their membership into two distinct groups, namely those entitled to wear "official clothing", or "livery" in Company colours and those who were not so entitled.

The livery men were usually drawn from those members who were in their early twenties, with capital and influence and who, after gaining experience under older men, had set-up in business on their own account. If they were successful as wholesalers they would be admitted to the livery at about the age of thirty or soon after. The group not admitted to the livery were generally those members who had not been commercially successful in the wholesale trade and had continued to depend on retail shopkeeping for their living.[6]

For those who have a deep interest in London and its medieval history, especially the mercers' trade, the history of the present day Smithfield area may be of interest. West Smithfield, the ancient Smethefielde or Smoothfield, is at the northern end of Giltspur Street. It was originally used for tournaments and executions and from the twelfth to the nineteenth century was the scene of the great cloth fair of St. Bartholomew, which in medieval times attracted buyers from all over Europe. The fair was stopped in 1870 because it had become "an increasing public nuisance".[5]

SOURCE REFERENCES

1. Sir Richard Whittington.
2. Medieval London, Discovering London 3.
3. The Model Merchant of the Middle Ages.
4. History of Henry IV.
5. Letts Visit London.
6. The Merchant Class of Medieval London.
7. Notes on Richard Whittington.
8. Guildhall Records Office: Husting Roll.
9. Mercers' Wardens Accounts.
10. Letter Books of the City of London.
11. Mercers' Acts.
12. Calendars of the Exchequer.

THE LEGISLATOR

Before going into Dick Whittington's activities as a City legislator, it is probably fitting to identify the various posts he held within the City of London. These, in summary, were: in 1385 and 1387 he sat in common council as the representative of Coleman Street Ward; in 1393 he was elected Alderman for the Broad Street Ward; from 1393 to 1394 he served as Sheriff to Mayor John Hadley, grocer;[1] on the eighth of June 1397 he was appointed Mayor of London by Richard II to fill the place of Adam Bamme, goldsmith, who died during his term of office. This latter appointment was to last until the next election.[2] In October 1397 he was elected Mayor for the following year with Sheriffs John Wodcoke and William Askam.[4] On the fifteenth of June 1400 Dick Whittington was present at a Privy Council meeting in the company of William Brampton and at that meeting it was suggested that he might be summoned to a great council in 1401.[3] In October 1406 he was elected Mayor for the ensuing year with Sheriffs Nicholas Wooton and Geffery Brooke. In October 1419 he was elected Mayor for the third full year of office with Sheriffs Robert Whityngham and John Butler.[4] In the Autumn of 1422 Dick Whittington attended the City elections for the last time. He died in early March 1423 having been overcome by the extreme cold weather of that winter[2] and possibly also becoming a victim of a severe form of influenza which was prevalent in the 1420s.[14] From memoirs in possession of the Mercers' Company it is recorded that, "The Company attended the cavalcade of Whittington chosen Mayor for the fourth time with eight new banners, eight trumpets, four pipes, seven nakerers".[2] A naker was a small kettle drum which came to England from Europe in the thirteenth century. It was usually played in pairs and accompanied dancing and chamber music and was also used on military occasions.[5]

Before the election of Dick Whittington to his second mayoralty a mass was held in the Guildhall chapel, after which the citizens made their nominations, "peaceably and amicably without any clamour or discussion". The custom, initiated by Whittington, of holding a religious service before the election of the Lord Mayor is observed to the present day. The title "Lord Mayor", only came into being at the end of the fifteenth century.[15]

The City records of 1418 show that Dick Whittington, Alderman, was present when it was agreed that the chaplain of the Chapel of Bones of the Dead in St. Pauls Churchyard, "who had exposed himself to manifold and constant anxieties for the good and honour of the chapel", should be presented with a gown of the same suit of livery as that given to the Sergeants of the Mayor.[10]

The election of Richard Whittington to his third mayoralty is recorded by Henry Thomas Riley in the following terms:—

"On Friday, the feast of St. Edward, the King and Confessor (thirteenth October) in the seventh year etc, after mass of holy spirit devoutly and becomingly celebrated with solemn music in a chapel of the Guildhall of the City of London, according to the ordinance made thereon in the time of John Woodcock, late Mayor of the said City, and approved, in presence of Mayor, Recorder, twenty-one Aldermen, two Sheriffs and an immense number of the Commonality of the citizens of the said City, summoned to the Guildhall of London for the election of the Mayor for the ensuing year, by their common assent, consent, and desire, Richard Whittington was chosen Mayor for the ensuing year; and on the morrow of the said feast was presented before the Barons of the Exchequer of our Lord the King, at Westminster, admitted and accepted as such."[6]

The "common councils" came into being as a direct result of the majority of the citizens becoming extremely dissatisfied with the City government and the standards being set by those in power. Rising prices were blamed on the Great Merchants and, in particular, on three Merchant Companies, the Vintners, the Fishmongers and the Drapers who in 1364 had bought Royal Charters granting them monopolistic rights. On the political side the impeachment of Aldermen Lyons, Peche and Adam de Bury was the last straw.[14]

Representatives of forty-one crafts were called to a council on the first of August 1376. At this meeting the three delinquent Aldermen were deposed and basic democratic principles were agreed, namely that there must be more citizen participation in civic government and that nothing should be done in secret by the Mayor and Aldermen. Councils, now termed "common councils", were to be elected annually from the crafts, were to meet at least twice a quarter and were to be responsible for the elections of Mayor and Sheriffs. A fresh council elected on the newly agreed rules and with representatives of fifty-one crafts attending was successful in November 1376 in obtaining a Royal Charter which forced Aldermen to retire after one year's service. This was too sweeping for some merchant dominated crafts and in March 1377 the Charter was modified to allow Aldermen to stand for re-election after a year's interval unless they had been found guilty of misconduct whilst in office. In 1379 the elected council was enlarged by the addition of "others of the more powerful and discrete citizens" and in 1380 there was a partial return to the original election by Wards. In the summer of 1384 a large council, packed for the occasion with a merchant majority, voted for returning to the original system of election by Wards. Finally a 1397 Ordinance deprived the citizens of the right to canvas in any Ward leaving the Mayor and Aldermen the sole right of final selection of potential council members. So an attempt to achieve a more democratic Ward structure was finally brought to nothing.[14]

In the early part of the fourteenth century, the ordinary costs of City government were not much in excess of one hundred pounds a year. Mayor and Aldermen served without salary but were allowed small privileges, such as enrolling their apprentices free and getting a free supply of water. The Mayor was also allowed to admit six men to citizenship, a right that was converted in 1434 into a present of four casks of wine.[16]

OTHER CIVIC DUTIES

Raising the City Militia

In July 1397 Dick Whittington was required to raise and assemble the City militia to accompany Richard II to Pleshy to arrest the Duke of Gloucester.[7] The "Lords Appellant" were a band of nobility who felt that they had been shut out of government and were frustrated, in their opinion, by the misgovernment and dictatorial approach of Richard II. The King considered these men a serious threat, particularly as they held considerable power with their own private armies and had parliament on their side. It was for this reason that the King acted against the Duke of Gloucester.[8] Dick Whittington was not a dedicated King's man because as the City militia went off to arrest the Duke of Gloucester he asked them most sincerely to pray not only for the King but also for the Duke and his followers.[19] This seeming paradox is very understandable when one realises that in these medieval times the nobility and the other educated portion of the population were very much concerned with the future of the soul and that everything should be done by those who were left behind to ensure that the dead should have a place in heaven. To emphasise this point it was the custom of the Mayors of Dick Whittington's time to hear mass with their complete retinue at least seven days in every year.[10]

The Prosecutor

In 1419/20 in his capacity as Mayor, Dick Whittington issued a proclamation against the mixture and adulteration of wines.[10] At the same time he was active against the forestallers, or wholesalers, of meat and sellers of dear ale.[11] In 1422 Dick Whittington laid information before the Mayor, Robert Chichley, against the Brewers' Company for selling dear ale. The Master and Wardens of the Company were convicted, fined twenty pounds and sent to prison in the Chamberlain's custody until the fine was paid.[17]

Dick Whittington's actions against the people who sold ale of poor quality and at too high a price was very important to the citizens of London as ale was in fact the only relatively cheap liquid that was safe to drink. The water was so polluted as to be virtually undrinkable and was, in effect, the cause of the many recurrent plagues that hit the country in these times. For example, a lesser known plague occurred in 1406 which killed more than thirty thousand people in London alone.[4] Setting the retail price for standard grades of ale, so as to minimise the tendency of prices to rise when supplies were short, was another of the Mayor's many responsibilities. Since ale was so important to commoner and nobility alike this mayoral duty was a very good test of his judgement and integrity. To assist the Mayor the City Corporation appointed an Ale Conner in each Ward who had to taste every brewing made for sale and assign it to one of the grades priced by the Mayor. Beadles checked the measuring vessels and were allowed to confiscate a third of any ale that was being sold dishonestly.[14]

The Ale Conner was reputed to wear leather breeches and, to test the quality of the ale, he was initially provided with two separate pints of ale. One pint he poured onto a bench and then sat in the puddle that it had created. He then drank the second pint and if, when the second pint was finished, his breeches stuck to the bench then the ale was considered to be up to standard![13]

Until the widespread use of hops, and the breweries delivered the ale to the inns and taverns, the ale was brewed by the tavern keeper's wife.[12] When the ale was brewed and ready to be sold the tavern keeper's wife would stick her ale-stake, or bush, into the front wall of the house as a sign and invitation to potential customers.[13]

Bakewell Hall

In 1397, when Dick Whittington was Mayor and in 1398 when Drew Barentin was Mayor, it was decreed that no foreigner, or stranger, was permitted to sell any cloth in the Bakewell Hall. The penalty was seizure of his goods. Bakewell Hall was, at that time, a weekly market for the sale of all kinds of woollen cloths, both broad and narrow.[4]

Prisons

In June 1419 the then Mayor, William Sevenoke, abolished Ludgate gaol and had the prisoners moved to Newgate. It was said that the privileges of Ludgate had been abused by persons "more willing to take up their abode there . . . than pay their debts". In November the same year, with Dick Whittington now Mayor, Dick ordered the use of Ludgate to be restored, since many had died in Newgate, "by reasons of the fetid and corrupt atmosphere that is in the hateful gaol of Newgate".[4]

SOURCE REFERENCES

1. Medieval London, Discovering London 3.
2. The Model Merchant of the Middle Ages.
3. Ordinances of the Privy Council, vol 1.
4. Survey of London.
5. Encyclopedia Britannica.
6. Memorials of London and London Life in the XIIIth, XIVth and XVth Centuries.
7. Annales Ricardi II (Rolls Series).
8. History of England.
9. Monasticon Anglicanum.
10. Sir Richard Whittington.
11. MS. Galba, B5.
12. Tudor London, Discovering London 4.
13. Life in Medieval England.
14. The Merchant Class of Medieval London.
15. Notes on Richard Whittington.
16. Calendar of Letter Books.
17. Old and New London.

THE FINANCIER

As a freeman of the City of London Dick Whittington was required to contribute in 1379 the sum of five pounds towards the defence of the City.[1] In 1389 the contribution had risen to ten pounds,[2] which indicates that his wealth had increased substantially in those ten years. The money was paid by Dick Whittington and other freemen to the City Chamberlain,[2] who in modern times would equate in duties and responsibilities to a City Treasurer.[3]

In 1358 City taxes were on a voluntary basis and only those failing to make a contribution were liable to assessment. In three assessments on goods and chattels in 1339, 1346 and 1376, exemption levels were set at forty shillings, ten pounds and ten marks respectively. The rate in a levy of one thousand pounds in 1371 was set at sixpence in the pound and to which was added in 1372 the sum of three shillings and fourpence for naval purposes.[14]

LOANS TO THE KING

In 1399 when Richard II was deposed and sent off to Pontefract to die, the King owed Dick Whittington one thousand marks which surprisingly was later repaid.[4] In Dick Whittington's time the rate of exchange seems to have been one and half marks equalling one pound sterling.[3] On the twenty-fourth of May 1400, Dick Whittington was authorised by Richard II to be paid the sum of one thousand pounds for goods supplied and past loans. Dick Whittington was to take this sum over the following three years from the Customs and subsidies on wools, hides and woolfells to be shipped by him through the Port of London.[13]

Dick Whittington also advanced, on loan, large sums of money to Henry IV and it is reported that on one occasion the sum involved was no less than six thousand four hundred pounds. Henry V borrowed money in order to carry on with his wars against the French and it is suggested that the King's bonds were bought up by Dick Whittington for the enormous sum of sixty thousand pounds.[5] Henry V's fund raising methods were certainly direct as can be judged from the following historical record:

On the tenth of March 1415 Henry V commanded Thomas Fauconer, the Mayor, and the Aldermen, and certain of the more substantial Commoners, to come to the Tower of London. He stated his reason as follows:—

"Well-beloved. We do desire that it shall not be concealed from the knowledge of your faithfulness, how that, God our rewarder, we do intend with no small army to visit the parts beyond the sea, that so we may duly reconquer the lands pertaining to the heirship and Crown of our Realm, and which have been for long, in the times of our predecessors, by enormous wrong withheld. But, seeing that we cannot speedily attain to everything that is necessary in this behalf for the perfecting of our wishes, in order that we may make provision for borrowing a competent sum of money of all the prelates, nobles, lords, cities, boroughs, and substantial men, of our Realm, we, knowing that you will be the more ready to incline to our wishes, the more immediately that the purpose of our intention, as aforesaid, rebounds to the manifest advantage of the whole Realm have therefore not long since come to the determination to send certain Lords of our Council unto the City aforesaid, to treat with you as to promoting the business before mentioned."[10]

However Henry V did show his appreciation to Dick Whittington, who was virtually acting as his banker, by entrusting him with the funds for the restoration of the nave of Westminster Abbey.[6] The King also forbade Nicholas Wotton, who was Mayor in 1415, from pulling down any building in the City without first consulting Dick Whittington and three others.[7] Dick Whittington seems to have returned the compliment, since it is said that on one occasion, when the King was returning from a victorious battle in France, Dick, with a cavalcade of City officials, met the King outside London and there tore up a bill from the King which amounted to thirty thousand pounds.[8]

The magnitude of Dick Whittington's loans far exceeded those made by any other London merchant and between 1388 and 1422 he lent money to the Crown on no less than fifty-eight occasions. For instance, in 1402 loans to the Crown totalled nearly five thousand pounds and in 1408 nearly three thousand seven hundred pounds.[12] In 1406 Dick Whittington received payment for two of the King's loans, one of £1,207.4s.0d. and the other of £2,015.3s.10d. The money came from the Collectors of Tenths for the Archdeaconries of Norfolk, Norwich, Suffolk, Sudbury and elsewhere.[13]

OTHER LOANS

According to the Chancery Extent for Debt, dated 1395, Philip Mansell, the brother of Dick Whittington's mother, had incurred a debt of five hundred pounds to Dick Whittington in February 1394 and which had remained unpaid by the due date of the first of April 1394. Philip's property was valued on the nineteenth of October 1395 and the manor of Over Lyppiatt, in Gloucestershire, was transferred to Dick Whittington for his use during his lifetime. On the nineteenth of December 1406 James Clifford, Esq. renounced his claim to the manor in favour of Dick Whittington, Sir William Hedyngton, Thomas Roos, Edmund Hodesdon and William Butt.[15]

It is said that Dick Whittington was defamed by a woman saying that he owed her money, jewels and goods worth many thousand marks. However she confessed that the charge was false and libellous and in truth she owed him money.[1] It is believed that Dick Whittington exercised clemency and that no action was taken against the woman concerned.

MAYOR OF THE STAPLE

During his lifetime and by Royal appointment Dick Whittington held the post of Mayor of the Staple of Westminster and Calais and also the position of Collector of the wool subsidies in London in 1401-3 and 1407-10. These positions gave him immense power both politically and in trade. For instance, on three occasions Dick Whittington was given a licence to export wool without paying any subsidy, until a royal debt had been discharged.[12]

From the late thirteenth century through to the sixteenth century, English wool exports were concentrated in one specific town which was called the Staple. The location of the Staple varied, but in the fourteenth century it was located at Calais with the object of reducing to a minimum the problems involved in collecting the export duties. The English merchants who controlled this export trade were called Merchant Staplers and were formally the Company of the Merchants of the Staple of which, as Mayor, Dick Whittington would have been a very important member. The Merchant Staplers were exerting their greatest influence in the fifteenth century having been granted, by the King, a monopoly over the export of wool and the collection of the duties. When the Staple was at Calais the Merchant Staplers were responsible for establishing trade regulations, administrating the merchant law in the city and they exercised political and diplomatic functions for the Crown.

With the growth of English manufacturing in the sixteenth century more wool was used for home industry and the export trade diminished and so also did the importance and influence of the Merchant Staplers.[9] However, in Dick Whittington's time this helped him to become wealthier and more powerful and also meant that he had very good basis for his many and sizeable loans to the Crown.

SOURCE REFERENCES

1. Sir Richard Whittington.
2. Memorials of London and London Life in the XIIIth, XIVth and XVth Centuries.
3. Medieval London, Discovering London 3.
4. History of Henry IV.
5. The Model Merchant of the Middle Ages.
6. Foedera.
7. Ordinances of the Privy Council.
8. Old English Customs and Ceremonies.
9. Encyclopedia Britannica.
10. They Saw It Happen.
11. The Merchant Class of Medieval London.
12. Notes on Richard Whittington.
13. Calendar to the Patent Rolls, Henry IV.
14. Calendar of Plea and Memoranda Rolls.
15. Public Records Office: Chancery Extent for Debt.

THE PUBLIC BENEFACTOR

ST. MICHAEL PATERNOSTER ROYAL

St. Michael Paternoster Royal was Dick Whittington's parish church and dated from about the middle of the thirteenth century. Its name was derived from two ancient thoroughfares, namely Paternoster Lane and La Riole. Royal is an anglicised version of La Riole which was a wine centre near Bordeaux with which the Vintners of the City of London traded.[1]

Dick Whittington lived just north of the church on what is presently known as College Hill. In his time this street was called Paternoster Street and it is assumed was originally Paternoster Lane.[1] His own house was purchased from Sir Baldwin Berford, Kt., on the twenty-second of February 1402.[13]

In Dick Whittington's opinion the existing church was too small and had become very dilapidated and so he took the following steps to acquire the additional land needed for the rebuilding. On the eighteenth of April 1409, Dick Whittington together with Henry London, his apprentice, and John Chamberleyn, chaplain, acquired from William Weston, draper, and Joan, his wife, land adjoining St. Michael Paternoster Royal.[13] On the twentieth of December 1409 these three persons obtained a Royal licence to grant the land to John White, parson, in perpetuity for the rebuilding of the church.[14] This grant was executed on the thirteenth of April 1411[15] and the rebuilding, which started soon afterwards, was continued throughout Dick Whittington's lifetime and completed by his executors after his death in 1423.

Dick Whittington provided a staff of thirty, which was composed of four Fellows, Clerks, Conducts and Choristers who were to pray for himself, his wife, Alice, and all his relatives. He not only paid the wages of the clergy but also provided funds for the continuing maintenance of the church.[2] Medieval London had in Dick

Whittington's time over one hundred churches which provided for some fifty thousand people. Since every Livery Company had its own church,[3] it is quite understandable that, as a respected mercer, Dick Whittington should have taken such a personal interest in the condition of his own parish church. Another reason for Dick Whittington's interest, and possibly a more compelling one, could have been his desire to provide a fitting burial place for his wife, Alice, who died in 1409, or thereabouts.

In 1630 the church was in need of repair and this was carried out for a sum of £120.9s.0d. and it is ironic that, after all Dick Whittington's efforts and following this repair in 1630, the church should have been totally destroyed in the Great Fire of 1666. The church was reconstructed between 1686 and 1694 by Edward Strong, Sir Christopher Wren's master mason, for £7455.7s.9d. It took a flying bomb on the twenty-third of July 1944 to finally undo all the past work. The church roof fell in and wrecked the interior of the church with the result that only the tower, which had been completed in 1713, and the walls remained standing.[1]

The present day association of the church with the "The Missions to Seamen" almost certainly has its origin in the Charter of the thirteenth of January 1394. The Mercers' Company, who obtained the Charter, were empowered, "to hold land for the benefit of those who by misfortune at sea and other casualties were so poor as to receive alms from other christian people".[16] Dick Whittington was elected Master of the Mercers' Company in June 1395 and therefore very probably had a hand in obtaining the Charter.[17]

GREY FRIAR MONASTERY LIBRARY

The Grey Friars were part of the Franciscan Order and their great church, which had been built in the early fourteenth century and destroyed in the Great Fire of 1666, was located on the north side of "The Shambles", which is now Newgate Street.[4] Dick Whittington's contribution was to found their library and the building, which was started in 1421, was completed in the following year. It was one hundred and twenty-nine feet long and thirty-one feet wide and panelled with wainscot. Twenty-eight desks were provided together with eight double settles, all constructed of wainscot which was a very fine grade of oak and derived its name from the Wainscot, or Panel, chair.[7] The cost of the building together with the books amounted to

Site of Dick Whittington's house on College Hill.

Church of St. Michael Paternoster Royal.

£556.10s.0d. of which four hundred pounds was paid by Dick Whittington and the balance by Dr. Thomas Winchelsey, a friar there. Other costs involved were the panelling of the choir at two hundred marks, painting at fifty marks and for writing out in two volumes the works of Nicholas of Lyra, and which were to be chained in the library, one hundred marks.[5]

The chief work of Nicholas of Lyra was the "Commentary Notes to the Universal Holy Scripture" in fifty volumes. This work was a "literal rather than a mystical or allegorical interpretation of the scriptures". It must have been, therefore, no mean feat to have condensed his works into two volumes.[6]

It is interesting to note that in these medieval days the Grey Friars were so revered that people had the strongest desire to be buried in their church and wrapped in the grey woollen shroud of the friars. No less than six hundred and sixty-three of the nobility, including four Queens, were buried in the church.[4] It is said that three of the four Queens were Queen Margaret of Anjou (Henry VI's wife), Queen Isabella of Spain and Mary Queen of Scots.[7]

LEADENHALL

The manor of Leaden Hall together with its endowments, went in 1380 from Alice Nevill, widow of Sir John Nevill, to Thomas Cogshall and others. In 1384 Humfrey de Bohun, Earl of Hereford, owned the manor and in 1408 the new owners, namely Robert Rikeden of Essex and Margaret, his wife, conferred on Dick Whittington and other citizens of London the manor together with its endowments of St. Peters Church, St. Margarets Pattens, etc.

In 1411 Dick Whittington and others gave the manor to the Mayor and Commonality of London and so it became part of, and belonged to, the City of London.[5]

Once in the possession of the City of London the manor became what we know today as Leadenhall Market.

Dick Whittington provided financial help in the building of the original Leadenhall Market[3] which was, in his day, a "foreign" market mostly used by country poulterers.[4]

John Stow, the sixteenth century historian, was buried in the church of St. Andrew Undershaft, Leadenhall Street and his monument is a bust which shows him writing in a book with a quill pen and with other books nearby. Each year the quill is replaced with a new one by the

Lord Mayor at an annual memorial service. A copy of Stow's works is awarded for the best essay on London written by a London scholar. The Headmaster of the winning pupil's school is given the old quill.[4]

THE "BOSSE" SPRING

Close by St. Giles Churchyard, Cripplegate, there was, in medieval times, a large pool in which, in 1244, Ann of Lodburie was said to have drowned. Shortly after, the pool was covered in but the spring which fed it was preserved. Stone steps were constructed leading down to the spring which was on the bank of the Town Ditch.[5] Dick Whittington provided a public "bosse", or water tap, in the east wall of the church of St. Giles, Cripplegate, so that the poor could be provided with free and unpolluted drinking water. The source of the water for this tap was from a conduit in Highbury.[2]

The Town Ditch was believed to have been first dug in 1213, but later excavations have proved that there was a Roman ditch there long before. Originally the whole length of the ditch, from the Tower of London to the river Fleet, was called "Hondesdich" or "Hundsditch", which in the course of time has become the present Houndsditch. Stow has suggested that the name came from the filth and, particularly, the dead dogs that were, from time to time, thrown in by the citizens of London.

The City records of the sixth of June 1532 decreed that this ditch must be cleaned up, the rubbish removed and no more thrown in.[4]

A present day visit to the church of St. Giles, Cripplegate, failed to discover any sign of Dick Whittington's public benefaction, although only the front, or west end, of the church has been rebuilt since the time of Dick Whittington.

CHAMBER AT THOMAS SPITAL

Dick Whittington provided a chamber, or room, at Thomas Spital with eight beds for young women "that had done amiss, keeping it a secret so no shame would stop their marriage".[8]

It is quite likely though that the Thomas referred to was the name of the hospital founded by the Canons of St. Mary Overie Priory in Southwark in the thirteenth century and named after Thomas Beckett, St. Thomas the Martyr. This supposition could very well be true since in medieval times a "spital" was a rest house, usually attached to a priory, for example, the spital of St. Mary's Priory, Billingsgate.[6]

Furthermore, William Gregory, writing some twenty or thirty years after Dick Whittington's death in 1423 described a refuge for unmarried mothers which Whittington added to St. Thomas' Hospital, Southwark.[12]

WESTMINSTER ABBEY NAVE

As has been mentioned earlier, Henry V entrusted Dick Whittington with the funds and the responsibility for the repair of the fabric of the Abbey and, in particular, the nave. The west end of the nave was built at least two centuries later than the east end. When the west end was built or repaired under the direction of Dick Whittington, the earlier style of architecture was copied so exactly that it is well-nigh impossible to tell where the work of Henry III left off and that of Henry V begins.[9]

PUBLIC LATRINE

In Dick Whittington's time every City Ward had a public latrine which was a step in the right direction so far as the public's health was concerned. For the smaller houses next-door neighbours shared the use of a privy but for the poor the streets of London had to serve.

In 1419, at Dick Whittington's expense, the finest public latrine of all was built in Vintry Ward at the northern end of Southwark bridge. This had sixty places for men and sixty places for women[3] and standing, as it did, beside the Thames, was purged at high tide. Above this public facility were provided five apartments for five pensioners of the parish.[11] It took the Great Fire of 1666 to bring an end to the particular grand public gesture.[3]

In 1690 the parishioners of St. Martin Vintry reminded the City Corporation of Dick Whittington's original benefaction which they termed the "Longhouse". The City Corporation responded by giving a hundred marks to rebuild the "Longhouse". However such a relatively small grant could only extend to providing places for six men and six women with no apartments above.[11]

BRIDGE AND CHAPEL AT ROCHESTER

In Richard II's reign (1377-1399), Sir Robert Knolles and Sir John de Cobham rebuilt the bridge across the river Medway at Rochester.[10] However, time and weather took its toll and Dick Whittington subscribed in his lifetime substantial sums to maintain the bridge and also the chapel at Rochester.[7] In the archives of the Rochester Bridge Trust is the following reference to Dick Whittington:—

> "Et de vijs. viijd. perditis in xl li. Receptis per Willelmum Sevenoke de Ricardo Hwytyngton . . . pro defectu ponderis."

The above entry relates to the accounts for 1422/23 and deals with the differences between the actual and the nominal value of various gifts.

It is not certain as to why Dick Whittington should have taken such an interest in Rochester, but when one remembers that he was much concerned with the church it begins to make possible sense. Also Dick Whittington would have been personally familiar with Chaucer and his Canterbury Tales. In fact before Chaucer lost the King's favour in 1387 and had turned to authorship to raise necessary finance, he had been, at different times, a respected courtier, diplomat, Member of Parliament and Controller of Customs.[19]

For pilgrims coming from the north and west, as well as from London, and going to Canterbury, it is almost certain that their route would have taken them across the Medway at Rochester. The pilgrims gathered in the inns and taverns at Southwark, which being outside the City walls meant that they could get an early start without waiting to have the City gates opened. The distance from Southwark to Canterbury is about sixty miles and would require at least one stopover for the pilgrims.[9] Chapels were normally built near bridges, particularly on pilgrim routes, and it was usual for the pilgrims to hear mass in the chapel.[3] It would also give them the chance of sanctuary overnight, since the highways and byways of medieval England were not particularly safe for travellers, even poor pilgrims.

GLOUCESTER CATHEDRAL

According to Samuel Lysons, Dick Whittington made substantial financial contributions to the repair and upkeep of the Cathedral fabric, especially the High Altar. Lysons also states that Dick Whittington watched the resulting expenditure with great care and interest.[1] Unfortunately the original High Altar of the Abbey church and its reredos were mutilated and almost certainly broken up by the iconoclasts in the time of Edward VI. Only the original stained glass window above the High Altar, known as the Crecy Window, still exists today with only some necessary repair work having been carried out

Embroidered cushion of Dick Whittington and his Cat.

Dick Whittington's tenement, Westgate Street, Gloucester.

since it was completed sometime between 1348 and 1350.[18] It is therefore unlikely that evidence of Lysons' assertions regarding Dick Whittingon's benefactions will ever be found in the Cathedral archives. There is, however, in the Cathedral one relatively modern visual connection with Dick Whittington. This is an embroidered cushion on the seat of the next but one choir stall beside the Bishop's seat which recalls the fable of Dick Whittington and his cat.

The interest that Dick Whittington had in Gloucester Cathedral is to be expected since his family were Gloucestershire based and he, himself, owned a tenement in Gloucester. The tenement was in Westgate Street, close by the Cathedral, and, having been classed as an historic building, has since been restored, at least on the outside. It is now a public house, called "Dick Whittington's House".

SOURCE REFERENCES

1. St. Michael Paternoster Royal—church pamphlet.
2. The Model Merchant of the Middle Ages.
3. Medieval London, Discovering London 3.
4. Tudor London, Discovering London 4.
5. Survey of London.
6. Encyclopedia Britannica.
7. Sir Richard Whittington.
8. Reign of Henry V.
9. In Search of London.
10. Life in Medieval England.
11. Guildhall Records Office: Viewer's Reports.
12. Historical Collections of a Citizen of London in the 15th Century.
13. Guildhall Records Office: Husting Roll.
14. Calendar to the Patent Rolls, Henry IV.
15. Calendar of Letter Book 1.
16. Calendar to the Patent Rolls, Richard III.
17. Mercers' Company: Wardens' Accounts.
18. Gloucester Cathedral—church publication.
19. The *Daily Telegraph*.

HIS LAST WILL AND TESTAMENT

Dick Whittington made his Will on the fifth of September 1421 and this was proved on the eighth of March 1423.[1] His executors were named as John Coventry, Mercer, Alderman and former Sheriff; John Carpenter, Town Clerk of London; John White, Master of St. Bartholomew's Hospital until the eighteenth of February 1423 (previously Rector of St. Michael Paternoster Royal until 1417);[7] William Grove.[2] A full text of his Will can be found in the Register of Henry Chichele, Archbishop of Canterbury, 1414-1443, vol.ii.

PERSONAL BEQUESTS

His personal bequests included the following:—

One penny to every man, woman and child on the day of his death. It is not certain whether this bequest referred to those living in the parish or only to those attending his funeral.[1]

Forty shillings each week to be distributed amongst the poor prisoners of Newgate, Ludgate, the Fleet, the Marshalsea and the King's Bench to a total of five hundred pounds.[7]

His house and other property in the City to be sold and the proceeds spent on masses to be said for the souls of himself, his wife, his father and mother and for all others to whom he was bound.[3] His City property included lands and tenements in the parishes of St. Andrew by Baynard Castle, St. Michael Bassieshaw and St. Botolph without Bishopsgate.[8]

To his older brother, Robert, he left a quantity of plate and other civic distinctions. These included "a collour of SS, 3 doz. sylver cupps with covers, the one doz. the second parcel gilt and the third white, 3 basins and ewers, 3 nests of bowls, 3 flagons and 3 livery pots all of the same material".[2]

To the Whittington Hospital he gave four mazers and twelve silver spoons with gilt knobs.[1]

His executors were instructed not to pursue any outstanding debts owed to him at his death and this instruction is described in Grafton's Chronicle in the following terms:—

"which also he willed to be fixed as a schedule to his last will and testament, the contents whereof was that if they found any debtor of his that ought to him any money, that if he were not in their consciences well worth three times as much, and also out of debt of other men, and well able to pay, that then they should never demand it, for he clearly forgave it, and that they should put no man in suit for any debt due to him".

Before Dick Whittington died, and in the presence of his executors, he made it clear to Thomas Roos that the manor of Over Lyppiatt and its lands were to be made over to his brother, Robert Whittington and his son, Guy. However Thomas Roos repeatedly refused to honour this bequest and the Whittington family were finally forced to go to the Court of Chancery claiming "that they had right and reason to the intent and will of the said Richard for God and as a work of charity". The petition was evidently successful and the Whittington family continued to hold this manor for more than a century.[6]

PUBLIC BEQUESTS

Having provided for his family during his lifetime Dick Whittington's executors were required to carry out the following actions using the considerable sum of money that he left and which amounted to between six thousand five hundred pounds and seven thousand pounds in liquid assets:—[5]

Found and build Whittington College together with a hospital or almshouse.[3]

Obtain a licence to rebuild Newgate gaol and see that the work was properly carried out.[1]

Repair St. Bartholomews Hospital in Smithfield[1] and found a library there.[2]

Glaze and pave the Guildhall.[1]

Finance the building of the Guildhall library.[2]

Finance the building of the West Gate of the City of London, the construction of which was started in 1422.[3]

HIS TOMB

Dick Whittington further directed in his Will that his body was to be interred on the north side of the high altar of his parish church, St. Michael Paternoster Royal.[4] His tomb was rifled in Edward VI's reign by the parson of the church, who imagined that there might be items of great value therein. This was not the case and so the parson took the only thing of value, which was the lead sheets in which Dick Whittington's body had been wrapped.

In the reign of Queen Mary (1553-1558) the parishioners were forced to wrap his body, as before, in lead sheets, replace his effigy and inter him for the third time.[3]

Acts of Court of the Mercers' Company of the twentieth of June 1569, the twenty-first of November 1616, the first of September 1654 and the twenty-third of May 1655 made reference to the repair of his tomb or banners.[9]

Dick Whittington's tomb was destroyed, with the church, in the Great Fire of 1666 and his body reinterred after the church was rebuilt.[4]

The flying bomb which severely damaged the church on the twenty-third of July 1944, and to which earlier reference has been made,[4] also wrecked the tombs of Dick Whittington and many other historically important persons. The devastation was so complete that the human remains could not be individually identified, so now they are sealed up in cement in a common grave under the church floor.

So after some five hundred and twenty-one years it may be said, with some degree of certainty, that the earthly remains of Dick Whittington will, at last, rest in peace.

SOURCE REFERENCES
1. The Model Merchant of the Middle Ages.
2. Sir Richard Whittington.
3. Survey of London.
4. St. Michael Paternoster Royal—church pamphlet.
5. The Charity of Richard Whittington.
6. Public Records Office: Early Chancery Proceedings.
7. Charities of London.
8. Guildhall Records Office: Husting Roll.
9. Mercers' Company : Acts of Court.

HIS EXECUTORS' ACTIONS

WHITTINGTON COLLEGE (COLLEGE of PRIESTS)

In 1411 Mayor Thomas Knoles, grocer, and the Commonality of London granted to Dick Whittington a vacant piece of ground on which to build his College in the Royal. This was confirmed by Henry VI in 1425 and again in 1432 by Parliament. It was suppressed by statute of Edward VI (1547-1553).[1]

On the twentieth of November 1424 his executors obtained the consent of the Archbishop of Canterbury to the collegiation of St. Michael Paternoster Royal. This consent was an Archiepiscopal peculiar.[2]

On the seventeenth of December 1424 the executors issued a Charter of Foundation and Regulations for a College dedicated to the Holy Ghost and the Virgin Mary.[2] The College was also known as St. Spirit and St. Mary[3] and was placed under the general supervision of the Mercers' Company.[4] The College and the Hospital, or Almshouse, shared a common chest in which was kept their common seals, their writings and privileges, their money and jewels. The chest had three locks, one key each to be kept by the Master or Tutor, another by the senior chaplain or almsman, and the third by one other chaplain or almsman to be appointed annually.[18]

The College was to consist of five priests, or chaplains, who were required to live in a newly built building at the east end of the church. They were required to say masses for the souls of Dick Whittington and his wife, his father and mother, Richard II, and Thomas of Woodstock and their wives.[2] The College was under the immediate supervision of the Master who was one of the five chaplains and elected at a meeting of their Chapter. The chaplains were also responsible for filling any vacancies in the College and if they failed in this duty after a maximum period of two months then the Mercers'

Company took over and made the necessary decisions.[18]

The Master received ten marks which were additional to other financial benefits arising out of his dual appointment of rector of St. Michael Paternoster Royal. The other chaplains received eleven marks a year, the senior clerk eight marks, the junior clerk one hundred shillings and the choristers five marks each. The choristers' annual pay was disbursed by the Master, or his deputy, for their food, clothing, teaching, shaving and washing. The priests received additional payment "for their attendance at the obits of Richard and Alice Whittington".[18]

On the thirteenth of February 1425 a further endowment was provided and rules added. In 1431 Reginald Pecock became Master.[2]

At the dissolution of the monasteries the College of Priests' buildings were granted to Armigale Wade, a clerk of the Privy Council, by Letters Patent dated the fourth of June 1548. The grant described the property as "the capital house and site of Whittington College with a porch and entry leading from the highway called The Royal and two chambers above the porch, a small garden abutting on the east end of the entry and a hall, a parlour, and a small garden adjacent to the hall". Wade was also to have all the goods and chattels on the premises, with the exception of any jewels or vessels of gold and silver. He paid £92.2s.7d. for the grant. In 1556 Wade sold the College to Sir John Wentworth of Gosfield, Essex for four hundred pounds and in 1559 John Wentworth, Esq. sold it to John Norris of Heywood, Berkshire, for the same price. In 1602 Sir John Norris sold it to the Skinners' Company for five hundred pounds. After the Great Fire the site became part of Skinners' Hall,[17] but its memory is kept alive today by College Street.[2]

Dick Whittington provided for the College an epitaph in latin verse, which described him as "Flos Mercatorum" and "Regia Spes et Pres" or "Flower of Merchants" and "Founder of Priests and Poor".[1]

WHITTINGTON ALMSHOUSE

On the twenty-first of December 1424 his executors founded an Almshouse (sometimes called a Hospital until the sixteenth century) which was located between the church of St. Michael Paternoster Royal, abutting the College of Priests, and Dick Whittington's house.[2]

After the Reformation it became customary to call the Almshouse the Whittington College. This title has been retained to present day, surviving subsequent moves to Highgate and then to Felbridge, East Grinstead.[18]

The Almshouse, or more correctly Whittington College, was restored after the Great Fire of 1666 for the sum of six hundred pounds, according to plans prepared by John Oliver, a City surveyor, and employing Barker (carpenter) and Metcalfe (bricklayer). The work started about October 1668 and was completed soon after January 1670.[18]

The Almshouse was founded for thirteen poor men of whom one was to be the Tutor.[2] The purpose of the hospital has been described by Wylie in the following terms:—

> "For such poor persons which grievous penury and cruel
> fortune hath oppressed and be not of power to get their
> living either by craft or by any other bodily labour."[3]

Only poor citizens of London were admitted and especially those of the Mercers' Company who were not of the livery. Livery men of any Company were excluded. The right to fill vacancies in the almshouse was shared by the Mercers' Company and the Master of the College of Priests who could claim every seventh nomination. If the Company and the Master failed to agree on any particular nomination, then the decision was left to the Mayor.[18]

On the thirtieth of March 1560 new ordinances were delivered to the Tutor on the orders of the Court of Assistance of the Mercers' Company. These ordinances, which had been amended when Elizabeth succeeded Mary on the throne, emphasised loyalty to the Crown and the reformed church. Each new inmate had to be examined by the Wardens of the Mercers' Company as to the articles of his faith, namely, "The Lord's Prayer and the Ten Commandments, all in English, and such other doctrine as is most necessary for every christian man". They also had to take an oath of loyalty to the Crown.[18]

Initially the almsmen were required to offer prayers for the souls of those persons referred to earlier in the description of the College of Priests.[2] However the aforementioned ordinances of 1560, no longer required daily attendance at mass or the offering of special prayers for the souls of the Founder, his family and benefactors.[18]

By the second of March 1711 it was noted by the Master and Wardens of the Mercers' Company that the inmates of the almshouse comprised one man, the Tutor, and twelve women. This was certainly not in accord with the original foundation of thirteen poor men and to achieve parity between the sexes it was ruled that a man should replace a woman on her death until there were at least six male inmates.[18]

Almsmen's Allowances

Initially the Tutor was to be paid sixteen pence a week and to be provided with a "little house with chimney con easement and other essentials to himself in which to lie and rest". The other twelve almsmen were to receive fourteen pence a week and be "provided with two meals a day together with over-clothing of a dark brown colour, not staring or blazing and of easy price according to their degree".[3]

In 1564 the weekly allowance was raised, in total, to forty-one shillings. A committee, appointed by the General Court on the fourteenth of August 1611 reported a week later that this allowance was sufficient subject to two provisions.

Firstly the custom of having no supper on Friday night was to be maintained and secondly that the weekly allowance was to be spent by the Tutor in the following manner:—

Item	a penny a piece a day in bread	6s.6d.
Item	four stone of beef	6s.0d.
Item	beer	8s.0d.
Item	milk and oatmeal	0s.15d.
Item	fish and roots three days	4s.0d.
Item	for six suppers	6s.6d.
Item	for conduit water, salt and herbs	0s.8d.
Item	to the dresser of their meat	0s.12d.
Item	for seacoals	0s.6d.
Item	for candles	0s.3d.
Item	for washing the house linen	0s.12d.
		a quarter
Item	for scavenge	0s.3d.

The balance of rather more than five shillings a week together with other private income and gifts would cover other essentials such as hose, shoes, linen and bedding.

Over the next sixty years the weekly allowance varied, sometimes up and sometimes down, according to the following schedule:—

May	1647	55/-
November	1650	48/-
November	1652	46/-
October	1666	23/-

This halving of the allowance in 1666 was the result of the Great Fire and the loss of revenue from property owned by the Mercers' Company. In addition the Mercers' Hall was destroyed and had to be rebuilt.

March	1667	39/-
October	1668	46/-
May	1671	50/-

Almsmen's Rules
These rules could be summarised as follows:—
— They could not leave the almshouse for a full day or go outside the parish without the Tutor's permission.
— They were forbidden to frequent taverns or wander idly in the streets. Sometimes such transgressions occurred under the pretence of going to listen to sermons being preached in City churches. The ordinances of 1560 reinforced this rule requiring the prior permission of the Tutor to attend such sermons.
— They were warned against drunkeness, gluttony and quarrelling amongst themselves.
— They were encouraged to quietly read, pray or work with their hands.

WHITTINGTON COLLEGE, HIGHGATE
The first positive step towards the building of a new and larger almshouse was taken by the Mercers' Company on the fifth of February 1818 when it was proposed to invest three thousand pounds of the surplus from the Whittington estate in Southsea stock as a rebuilding fund.

A committee was set up to make recommendations as to the number of residents, their allowances and the overall costs in relation to the available capital. As regards the location of the new building, the Mercers' Court instructed the committee to purchase sufficient land as close as possible to Whittington's Stone on the south side of Highgate Hill. The original stone marked, according to tradition, the place where Dick Whittington, a poor apprentice, heard Bow Bells and returning to London found fame and fortune. The chosen site belonged to the Highgate Archway Company and the Mercers' Company obtained Letters Patent granting them a licence to hold the land in "mortmain" on the twentieth of December 1822 and the lease was executed on the first of January 1823. The land was later purchased outright by the Mercers' Company. The original College site on College Hill became a school which was opened in 1832 and continued there until 1894 when it was moved to Barnard's Inn, Holborn.

The plans for the new College were drawn up by George Smith of Bread Street, the Mercers' surveyor, and provided for thirty houses for the almspeople and a chapel. Sixteen building tenders were submitted on the first of July 1822, ranging from thirteen thousand and twenty-nine pounds to nine thousand six hundred and sixty-three pounds. The lowest tender, submitted by Thomas Phipp and George Ward of Bennett Street, Blackfriars Road, was accepted and the contract signed on the twenty-ninth of August 1822. Building progressed slowly until January 1824 when some minor modifications were agreed. The original decision to provide coppers for each house was revoked on the grounds of expense and the likelihood of them being stolen and an iron pot substituted. Cottage stoves were to be provided in the lower room and bath stoves in the upper room of each house at an additional cost of £325.4s.0d. which also included a knocker for the front door of each house. A reading desk and movable seats, with backs, were to be placed in the chapel. To provide a ready source of fresh water at an economical cost, two underground tanks and the necessary pumps were provided. On the eighth of July 1824 the building was complete and ready for occupation but the actual move did not take place until September. The final cost amounted to £13,494.2s.10d. which was rather more than the original contract price. However nearly one thousand pounds was spent on excavation and nearly two thousand pounds on additional foundation work.

In October 1824 the garden was laid out and in December an eight-day turret clock was bought from Robert Gauthony. During the winter of 1825-6 a cottage was built for the gardener and in April 1826 a statue of Dick Whittington, by Joseph Carew, was purchased for fifty guineas and placed in front of the College. A report on the twenty-eighth of July 1831 enumerated various serious building defects, including use of inferior bricks, crumbling mortar, roof tiles overhanging too small gutters, and rot in the floors and joists. However the Mercers' Court of Assistance took no action as they probably thought it unlikely that they could get any redress from the builder. Some later modifications were made, such as facing the buildings with

Portland cement in 1830, laying on a water supply to each house in 1862 and providing each house with an additional bedroom in 1877.

Numbers of Pensioners

On the twentieth of December 1821 it was proposed by the Mercers' Company that the number of residents in the new building should be thirty-six and also an equal number of annual out-pensions should be granted. The residents would comprise thirty-five women with one man as Tutor. The out-pensioners could be either men or women and no almsperson under the age of fifty-five could qualify for residency or for an out-pension. Nominations for places in the College and for out-pensions were made by members of the Court of Assistance in order of seniority and the actual appointments were made by the Master and Wardens of the Mercers' Company.

When the committee, appointed by the Mercers' Company, made its report on the fifth of February 1822, it was pointed out that the total financial burden would absorb nearly all the income from the Whittington estate. The committee strongly recommended that the total numbers of both residents and out-pensioners should be reduced from thirty-six to thirty. This would not only reduce the amount to be paid in annual allowances but would also make a substantial saving in building costs. The committee's report was approved on the twenty-first of February 1822 and they were asked to put their proposals into effect.[18]

Allowances to Pensioners

The proposals made, and accepted, in February 1822 granted an annual allowance of thirty pounds to residents and out-pensioners alike and the first payment was made on the second of October 1824.

For an out-pensioner to qualify he or she could not have an annual income of more than twenty pounds from real-estate or thirty pounds from any other source. Also the pensioner must live within ten miles of London and no servants were eligible as long as they remained in service. The pensions were renewed annually by the Court of Assistance and the pensioner had to send annually an affidavit to the Clerk of the Mercers' Company stating that he or she were conforming to the Company regulations.

The regulations were revised in May 1867 raising the income limit to forty pounds a year from any source and in June the residential qualification was withdrawn.

An increase in income from the Whittington estate made it possible to increase the number of out-pensioners from thirty to sixty as from January 1867. Further increases in numbers of pensioners and allowances occurred as follows:—

16 April 1875   All pensions increased from thirty pounds to thirty-five pounds a year.

Number of out-pensions increased by forty-five.

1878   Residents' pensions increased to forty pounds a year.

Number of out-pensions increased by twenty-five at thirty-five pounds a year.

January 1884   Out-pensions increased to forty pounds a year.

Number of out-pensions increased by thirty.

June   1884   Number of out-pensions increased by sixty.

By 1908 the number of out-pensioners had risen to two hundred and eighty and then dropped to two hundred and sixty-five by 1949. On the seventeenth of June 1949 an application was made to the Charity Commissioners to amend the Scheme of Management of 1909 to allow the number of out-pensions to be run down until it reached two hundred in about 1952.[18]

Rules for Presidents

In July 1824 the following new rules for the conduct of the residents were approved:—

"The tutor was to be a poor middle-aged clergyman and was to be allocated one of the houses adjoining the road. He was to be in constant residence and to have the general supervision of the whole establishment. He was to perform the full church service and to preach in the chapel every Sunday morning at eleven o'clock. He was to visit the sick and provide spiritual consolation for the inmates at large. He was to have the key of the gate opposite his house and to keep the gate locked from ten at night until seven in the morning during the summer and from nine at night until eight in the morning during the winter. He was to receive the allowances for the whole establishment monthly at the Mercers' Hall and to distribute the money the same day. He was to keep a daily common place book for everything worthy of record, especially noting cases of improper conduct, such as residents who did not come home before the gates were locked and residents who did not attend chapel. This book was to be shown to the Master and Wardens of the Company once a year. The Tutor was given authority to grant occasional leave of absence, not exceeding six weeks a year, to the almswomen. Such grants must be recorded in the common place book. If the Tutor himself required leave of absence he had to obtain licence from the Master and Wardens and provide someone to officiate in his place."

The rules also laid down that one of the almswomen was to be appointed Matron by the Court of Assistance.

"She was to receive an annual salary of £52.10s. and was, like the Tutor, to occupy a house adjoining the road. She was also to be in constant residence and to have the general supervision of the College, with the Tutor. She too was to have the key of the gate opposite her house, which was to be locked at the same hours as the gate opposite the Tutor's house. She was not to permit access to the College after the gates had been locked and was to report to the Tutor the names of those absent without leave after the gates had been shut, as well as any other breach of the rules by the inmates. It was her duty to examine the interior of every house, except the Tutor's, once a month to see if they were clean and in good order. She was to send for the apothecary whenever any of the almswomen were ill and to see that the patients were properly attended, as well as appointing and directing the duties of the two visiting nurses. She must also see that no dirt or rubbish was thrown into the area in front of the College and that no washing or domestic work was done there on any pretence whatsoever. Finally, after the death of any of the almswomen, she was responsible for seeing that the dead woman's house was washed and purified before being re-occupied."

"The resident almswomen were to be single women or widows over fifty-five years of age without income exceeding fifty pounds a year, exclusive of the allowance granted by the Company from the Whittington estate. They were to reside constantly in the houses allotted to them and would be in the College each night before the gates were locked. Each woman was expected to keep her own house clean, scouring the floors, stairs and passages at least once a month. She must sweep the paved terrace in front of her house every morning before twelve o'clock and have her bedstead pulled down and the joints and headrails well washed every April. She had to pay for any windows in the house which might break and she was forbidden to drive any nails, hooks or screws into the walls. She must do her washing and other domestic chores either inside or at the back of her house. She was expected to attend service in the chapel every Sunday morning unless she was ill or absent with leave. All the almswomen were enjoined to be clean in their persons, regular in their habits and civil and respectful in their conduct with each other. They must observe the rules or risk dismissal."

"As for any almswomen who were ill a local apothecary was appointed to visit them daily at the request of the Matron and to supply the necessary medicines. In addition, two of the most active and healthy of the almswomen were to be nominated each year by the Master and Wardens to act as visiting nurses for that year. Each nurse was to receive an allowance of ten pounds for the year. One was to be responsible for the fifteen houses north of the chapel, the other for the fifteen houses south of the chapel. The nurses' duties consisted of visiting the sick at least once a day and administering medicines and performing such services as were requested by the Matron. They also had to keep the chapel and the pump yards clean and to wash the Tutor's surplice and the chapel linen. They must see that all the chimneys were swept by a machine once every three months and they were 'not to permit climbing boys to be employed in any case whatever'."

In spite of the evident care with which the rules were drawn up they didn't seem to be particularly effective. Within ten years the Master and Wardens were able to report that they had looked up the rules made when the College moved to Highgate and found that they had never generally been made known or acted upon. Their major problem

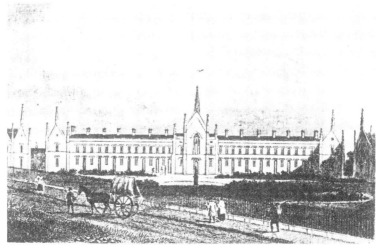

Whittington College, Highgate, 1827.

Whittington College, Felbridge.

was the inadequacy of the nurse. Ignoring the regulations about nursing staff laid down in 1824 the wife of the gardener had been appointed nurse to the College. Because she had a husband and a family to look after, she could not give her undivided attention to the almswomen and the Master and Wardens recommended the appointment of a Matron and of a nurse to live either with the Matron or in the house of the almswoman needing most attention. There was usually one inmate who was confined to bed and this meant that the nurse could occupy the lower room of the house in question. These recommendations were put into effect in July 1833 and the gardener was compensated for the loss of income resulting from the dismissal of his wife.

In 1879 the rules of the College were revised and based, in part, on suggestions made by the Tutor. He felt that the residents of the College should no longer be called almswomen, "the name did not accord with the type of women now being admitted and wounded their feelings". He suggested that "resident pensioners" would be more suitable. He thought that the name of Tutor should be changed to chaplain as the word "Tutor" was misleading. He pointed out that when the office was last vacant the notice advertising the post had been inserted in the paper among the scholastic advertisements because that had seemed the most fitting place to the proprietors of the paper. He also asked that the Tutor might be allowed to authorise females to reside in the College as companions to the inmates, providing that they conformed to regulations laid down by the Court of Assistance. If it was necessary for men or children to reside in the College, permission must be given by the Master or Wardens as he was anxious to safeguard against the residents taking in lodgers. Finally, he proposed that the detailed rules for the servants should be omitted as he felt that good order and regularity would best be observed by the absence of any defined limits to the obedience which they were required to render to the Matron or Tutor. The Tutor pointed out that these proposals did not change the substance of the rules, but merely removed what had become obsolete. The Master and Wardens did not feel that they could go as far as the Tutor wished, since, in their opinion, it was not desirable to alter the form of the rules and regulations. The name "Tutor" had been in use since the time of Whittington and there was no reason to change it now. The Master and Wardens did agree that the inmates should no longer be called "almswomen" but "resident pensioners" and they approved the suggestion that the residents should be allowed to have female companions. They also reaffirmed their former opinion that the residents need not attend church services every day.

The arrangement with regard to the female companions lasted only until 1883. On the sixth of July 1883 the existing rules regarding visitors, having proved to be outdated, were revised as follows:—

> "any resident could have a visitor to stay the night with the consent of the Tutor or Matron. Visitors must not stay more than fifteen days without special permission, though they could stay for up to six weeks if this permission was obtained. If a resident wanted a family relative or friend to stay for longer than six weeks she must apply through the Tutor to the Master and Wardens."[18]

WHITTINGTON COLLEGE, FELBRIDGE

A 1962 decision by the Ministry of Transport to widen Highgate Hill as part of a scheme, known as the Archway Road Intersection, caused the Mercers' Company actively to seek a new site for the Whittington College.[18]

The present-day Whittington Hospital, "The Hospital on the Hill", opened in 1948, was the result of combining three long-existing workhouse infirmaries and was unaffected by the proposed widening of Archway Road. The chosen name for the hospital was considered an improvement on the alternative name, "Trinity", in view of its location and associations with Dick Whittington, both fact and fable.[19]

Accordingly the College at Highgate was sold for about two hundred and fifty thousand pounds and work started on a new College at Felbridge, near East Grinstead, in September 1965. The College, which is administered by the Mercers' Company in their capacity as Trustees of the Almshouse Charity founded under the Will of Dick Whittington, was completed and ready for occupation one year later. The move to Felbridge actually took place on the twenty-ninth of September 1966. The College, which has been described as "a village within a village", initially comprised twenty-eight two-bedroomed self-contained bungalows for the resident pensioners together with separate houses for the Tutor, Matron, Assistant Matron and gardener.[18]

In 1978 the residential accommodation was enlarged by the addition of seven bungalows, specially designed for married couples, together with some twelve one-bedroomed flats and bedsitters, all under one roof in a single-storey building. Some four years later the "sheltered" accommodation was itself extended and raised the total number of flats and bedsitters from twelve to twenty-four. The flats and bedsitters are grouped around an ambulatory with a fountain and, like the bungalows, each has a small, but well-stocked and attractive garden bed outside each front door. The original twenty-eight bungalows were provided with a communal and fully equipped laundry and dispensary. The flats and bedsitters all have their own separate kitchen, together with a communal laundry, a resident nurse at each end of the building and a surgery. The College doctor holds a surgery every Friday to treat those residents in need and so save them having to go out in all weathers.

As can be judged considerable thought has been put into the question of the care, and comfort, of the residents, but there is much more to tell. For those in the flats and bedsitters, being without a spare bedroom, accommodation is provided for the overnight stay of their visitors and thus gives a degree of equality of circumstances with those who have been allocated bungalows. All accommodation has central heating and most have their own telephone and television. The residents are expected to provide their own furniture and thereby give an important personal ingredient to a life which otherwise might be somewhat withdrawn and institutional. However, should any incoming resident be in financial difficulties the Mercers' Company would help that person, both practically and financially, to obtain those items which were needed and which were of the individual's choice.

Movement from the "sheltered" accommodation into the bungalows is not the policy of the College since otherwise there would be "general post" every time someone died. However the reverse can apply when a resident in a bungalow is feeling their age and a flat becomes vacant.

The Chapel is the focal point of community life and was originally built with a seating capacity of forty-eight. It has had to be enlarged in line with the increased number of bungalows and the provision of "sheltered" accommodation. This extension was completed, and the Chapel re-hallowed by the Bishop, in 1984 and can now comfortably accommodate all those at the College, staff and residents alike. The Chaplain, who is also the Tutor, is an ordained Minister of the Church of England and has, therefore, responsibility under the overall supervision of the Mercers' Almshouse Committee for the residents' spiritual and secular welfare. There is no laid down period of time governing the Tutor's appointment but a five-year term would appear to be the present-day norm for a man who is required to be all things to all people in this rather unusual community. When the Chapel was enlarged the original organ, which was brought from Highgate, was replaced by a new electronic one.

All that has been described is contained within an area of some thirty acres. There are magnificent and stately trees, some of which have their individual ages counted in hundreds of years, and wooded areas of wild daffodils and bluebells. Mellowed brick walls support espaliered trees and the many small gardens outside every bungalow, flat and bedsitter are, in season, a mass of colour, including azaleas and roses. Not surprisingly there are now two full-time gardeners employed to maintain this well-ordered acreage of peace and beauty.

Joseph Carew's statue of Dick Whittington, which was brought from Highgate, stands at the entrance to the College and a very much smaller version, in a glass dome, can be seen on one of the Chapel window ledges. The Whittington coat of arms is on each of the two chairs either side of the altar. It is also on the kneelers at the communion rail, and on the chair cushions, these having been worked by several of the residents.

Residency Qualifications

To be considered for admission applicants must:—

(i) Be retired professional or business women or widows of men from a similar background (or married couples) who are in reduced circumstances and have a real housing need.

(ii) Be communicant members of the Church of England.

(iii) Be aged fifty-five years or over.

(iv) Be in good health and able to look after themselves in every way.

Of those who apply and who are subsequently "elected" to the College some have a missionary background and others have also spent their professional working life in "tied" accommodation in this country or abroad. The latter category could, for instance, include Matrons of nursing homes, private secretaries and clerks. Of course in this imperfect world there will always be some whose lives have collapsed around them and require to be looked after in a supportive community.

A connection with the Mercers' Company is not a prerequisite for election to the College although such an association would be a point in an applicant's favour. Now, in 1987, there is one resident whose husband was a mercer and another whose father was a mercer. It is getting increasingly difficult to "elect" people to the College, partly due to the financial and housing requirements of "need" and to the availability of appropriate accommodation. At the present time governmental housing density regulations for the area virtually decree that there can be no further extension to the existing establishment. Also the Mercers' Company is firmly against turning away suitable applicants or instituting some form of waiting list so they try to strike a balance between suitably qualified applicants and the type of accommodation available at the particular time. Of course the Mercers' Company is dealing with people and their diverse situations so an exact balance cannot always be achieved.

No single men are admitted and to date no wife of a residential couple has predeceased her husband.

Election Procedure

The first step to be taken by aspiring applicants is to apply to the Clerk to the Mercers' Company at Mercers' Hall stating their situation and need. These applications are then reviewed by the Almshouse Committee and likely persons, in relation to the accommodation available, called to the next stage.

The second stage involves attending the College and undergoing an examination by the College Medical Officer. This College visit gives both staff and applicant a chance to make their own individual assessments of the College's aim to maintain a happy integrated community in conformity with the necessary rules and type of accommodation available at the time. Basically a vacancy occurs when a resident dies but in practice there are additional reasons such as failing health requiring nursing home care or a simple wish to leave.

The third and final step is an interview at Mercers' Hall conducted by the members of the Almshouse Committee who have the College medical report in their possession. Normally the applicant will be advised by letter as to whether or not she has been elected to the College. However, if there is no competition, such as only one person after one bungalow, or flat, then they may well be told at the conclusion of the interview. It should be said that in the case of married couples, both husband and wife are considered to be separate entities as regards admission to the College. In other words they must each meet the residency qualifications and each must pass the three distinct selection states. A husband cannot become a resident simply by his wife being successful. However, if the husband dies after the couple has been granted a married quarter, then the widow would be allowed to stay on in the bungalow.

Allowances to Residents

From the Whittington Trust some residents receive a pension which is quite separate from any State pension or other allowance. From the resident's total income only the cost of food, clothing, telephone, outings, holidays and other personal expenses have to be met. Heating, television licence and window cleaning, are at present free. Lighting is also free in the flats.

Every resident receives a Christmas hamper from the Mercers' Company and also a gift of tea about the middle of the year when the Master and Wardens of the Mercers' Company visit the College.

Medical care is free and includes the services of the College doctor, Matron, nurses and a visiting physiotherapist. Should a resident's health fail to the extent that keeping her house truly clean and tidy becomes too burdensome then the College will provide, without charge, such domestic help as is needed.

This total removal of financial worry when taken into consideration with the living conditions, as already described, has continued to create a very happy community. Of course in any community some are more public minded than others but nobody can pretend that they can change human nature however idyllic the conditions may be.

REBUILDING OF NEWGATE GAOL

The first prison on the site was the "New" City Gate, filled to overflowing in the twelfth century, and notorious for its corrupt gaolers. The prison was wrecked by Wat Tyler and his men in 1381.[7]

A rebuilding licence was obtained in 1422 on the grounds that the existing gaol was too small and sufficiently infected as to cause many deaths amongst the inmates. The necessary rebuilding work was carried out under the inspection of Dick Whittington's executors using the legacies left in his Will.[6]

The rebuilt gaol was greatly damaged by the Great Fire in 1666 and again in 1780 by an anti-catholic mob of fifty thousand led by Lord Gordon. In 1783 the City architect, George Dance, built a new prison, which the Westminster magistrate, Henry Fielding (author of "Tom Jones"), called the "Prototype of Hell". After that, condemned prisoners were no longer hanged in front of the crowds at Tyburn (now Marble Arch) but executed outside the prison until 1868.[7]

Throughout those years when the condemned men were hung at Tyburn a hand bell was rung outside their cells at midnight[7] and the following verses recited:—

"All you that in the condemned hole to lie,
Prepare you, for tomorrow you shall die;
Watch all and pray; the hour is drawing near.
That you before the Almighty must appear.

Examine well yourselves; in time repent.
That you may not to eternal flames be sent.
And when St. Sepulchre's Bell in the morning tolls
The Lord above have mercy on your souls.

PAST 12 O'CLOCK."[8]

On the following morning, the day of execution, each prisoner, starting on the long walk to the gallows at Tyburn, would stop at the church of St. Sepulchre to receive a blessing and a nosegay from the priest.[7] The actual bell is now in the church of St. Sepulchre which is located on the corner of Giltspur Street and Holborn Viaduct. This custom, carried out by the Bellman of St. Sepulchre, originated in a gift, or bequest, of fifty pounds which was made by Robert Dowe in 1605.[8]

The Central Criminal Court (the Old Bailey) now stands on the site of Newgate Prison which was pulled down for the last time in 1902.[7]

ST. BARTHOLOMEW'S HOSPITAL

St. Bartholomew's Hospital was originally governed by a Master, eight brethren (priests) and four sisters and was for the poor and diseased.[1] The Hospital and its associated church of St. Bartholomew the Great originally formed part of an Augustinian priory, which was founded in 1123 by Rahere, a favourite courtier of Henry I. In the priory church can now be found the tomb and effigy of Rahere, the founder and first Prior.

On the same side of the street as the church of St. Sepulchre was a house from which a watch used to be kept on the graveyard. This watch was necessary to prevent the students from the Hospital, located across the street, from plundering it for anatomical specimens.[7]

The Hospital was repaired in about 1423 at a time when physicians and surgeons were scarce. Dick Whittington's posthumous contribution to the Hospital was the foundation of a library and the building of the great South Gate.

As regards the founding of the library, the Cartulary of the Hospital contains no record of furniture or other domestic property of the hospital except the books in the list of Masters in the paragraph concerning John Wakering.[15] This reference clearly indicated the existence of a well established library by the year 1463. A further reference records the remains of the library being sold in 1549. From the aforementioned sale the Treasurer received one pound for old books, ten shillings for a book "boxed and bounde to register the Treasurer's accomptes in", and three shillings and ten pence for a "reame of writing paper".[15]

The work undertaken by Dick Whittington's executors in building the great South Gate was in compensation for an annual quit-rent of twenty shillings on his house in La Riole received by the Hospital.[16] The Gate, as finally built, included a stone column with arms of Dick Whittington, an arch in the wall adjoining the chapel of St. Nicholas and a "glass window, with its tracery, representing the seven corporal works of Mercery". The mason's work cost sixty four pounds out of a total cost of £174.14s.4d.[15] This total amount was considerably more than the value of the quit-rent but John White, one of Dick Whittington's executors, had been Master of the Hospital until the eighteenth of February 1423 and had occupied Dick Whittington's house after the latter's death in early March 1423.[16]

GUILDHALL—PAVING AND GLAZING

Based on voluntary donations an extension to the Guildhall was begun in 1410 but funds ran short in 1413. The money required to complete the work was then financed by raising the Guildhall fees for the enrolment of Wills and Deeds, the registration of apprentices and use of the Mayor's seal and by drawing on the revenues from London Bridge.[14]

Paving

To further improve the appearance of the Guildhall, Dick

Whittington, in 1422, gave twenty pounds towards paving the Guildhall and fifteen pounds more in the next year for the provision of the hard stone of Purbeck.[1] From the thirteenth century onwards the best known English quarries, such as Corfe, York and Burton, set up workshops for the prefabrication, in Purbeck marble, of statues, tombs, columns, etc. These were normally provided in standard patterns, but the quarries would also cut stones to specific designs. The Purbeck marble was greatly in demand since it was considerably cheaper than the imported French equivalent.[10]

Glazing
A fifteenth century window exists today and is located in the south wall of the Guildhall. The panes in the window are of horn, instead of glass,[11] which was relatively expensive. During the fourteenth and fifteenth centuries the wealthy merchants used glass in preference to horn, which apart from the expense, was not opaque but clear.[10]
For the glazing of the Guildhall, coloured glass was used by his executors and on every window of the Mayor's Court were placed the arms of Dick Whittington.[1]
In the fourteenth and fifteenth centuries English white glass cost about four or five pence a square foot. Coloured glass was at least three times and often six times as expensive. The cost of coloured glass was high because of transport costs from Normandy or the Rhineland. English glass makers could not offer coloured glass at competitive prices until the latter half of the fifteenth century.[12]

GUILDHALL LIBRARY
In accordance with Dick Whittington's Will, his executors, in association with those of William Bury, mercer, founded a library for the Guildhall with the executors paying half the cost of the building. On one side, the arms of Dick Whittington were cut into the stone work and on the other side were the two letters, W and B, which stood for William Bury. Sometime after the library was completed it was lofted through and made into a part store house for clothes.[1]
The books in the library were "borrowed" by the Duke of Somerset in the reign of Edward VI (1547-1553).[9]
The Great Fire of 1666 virtually destroyed the Guildhall and only left the crypt, porch and walls still standing.[13] The crypt is the earliest part of the building to survive and this was begun in 1411. The Great

Guildhall.

Original 15th century horn window.

Hall was completed by 1440.[11] In the Great Hall marks on the stonework from the Great Fire of 1666 are still visible to this day.

Prior to the 1940 blitz on London, the library books with a financial value had been removed from the library and put into safe-keeping. As a result of the blitz, three bays at one end of the library were destroyed together with the books which had been retained and which were primarily for student research. In the view of Mr. Douthwaite, the then Librarian, the student books were irreplaceable and of far more benefit to future generations than the ones of financial value. Sad to say this wartime destruction of parts of the Guildhall need not have happened. The roof of the Guildhall was initially set alight as a result of sparks blowing from the church of St. Lawrence Jewry and an inadequate fire watch on the church itself.[13]

When the Guildhall was well alight and the burning roof fell in, part of the original medieval crypt was destroyed. However, a substantial part of the original crypt remains to this day. In Dick Whittington's time the floor of the crypt was at the original street level and this is why the Guildhall crypt, unlike any other, is provided with windows. The original outer columns, forming the outer wall, have grooves, at two different levels, worn in them. It is believed that these grooves were formed in medieval times when the horses, bringing the Mayor and his retinue to the Guildhall, were tethered there.

Since the last war considerable rebuilding and extension work has been carried out on the Guildhall. A new library was built about 1974 and the books removed from the "old" library. The original carved wooden bookcases, dating from the rebuilding after the Great Fire of 1666, have been removed, crated up and sold to the United States of America.

So the "old" Guildhall library no longer exists as a library, but remains as a grand meeting place and for the holding of special functions. At the north end of the "old" library there is a magnificent stained glass window which depicts many past Mayors of London. Dick Whittington is included in this great window, so his original benefaction has not been totally lost, even though the library that he originally provided has been devastated by two great fires.

SOURCE REFERENCES
 1. Survey of London.
 2. Monasticon Anglicanum.
 3. Reign of Henry V.
 4. St. Michael Paternoster Royal—church pamphlet.
 5. The Mercers' Company of the City of London and its Hall.
 6. The Model Merchant of the Middle Ages.
 7. Letts Visit London.
 8. Church of the Holy Sepulchre, London—Execution Bell.
 9. Sir Richard Whittington.
10. Life in Medieval England.
11. Medieval London, Discovering London 3.
12. Encyclopedia Britannica.
13. In Search of London.
14. The Merchant Class of Medieval London.
15. The History of St. Bartholomew's Hospital.
16. St. Bartholomew's Hospital Records: Cartulary of John Cok.
17. Calendar of Records of the Skinners' Company, January 1965.
18. The Charity of Richard Whittington.
19. The Hospital on the Hill.

POSTSCRIPT

Since so much of the physical evidence of Dick Whittington's, and his executors' public benefactions was destroyed by the Great Fire of 1666, it is fitting that some details of the fire should be given.

In the early hours of Monday, the second of September, 1666, a chimney fire in a baker's house in Pudding Lane spread to the adjoining house and then, fanned by an east wind, to Thames Street. Having reached Thames Street, the fire set alight tallow, corn, spirits and coal. By this time, the fire was completely beyond the control of human bucket chains from the nearest conduits, and the Lord Mayor would not permit the use of hooks on long poles to create fire gaps since he was afraid of accepting the responsibility for destroying, or at least badly damaging, the houses of influential citizens. However the King ordered whole streets to be blown up to control the spread of the fire.[1]

The wind dropped late on Tuesday night effectively bringing the devastation to a halt but still leaving three-fifths of the City a smoldering ruin. The financial loss was estimated at the staggering sum of three and a half million pounds.[1]

To the east, and at a distance of two hundred and two feet from the origin of the fire, there now stands, in commemoration, the Monument which, logically, is two hundred and two feet high. On the north side of the base of the Monument can be found, in Latin, the detailed statistics of an inferno which lasted less than forty-eight hours. Below the Latin inscription, carved in the stone, is a plaque providing an English translation which reads as follows:—

> In the year of Christ 1666, on the 2nd September, at a distance eastward from this place of 202 feet, which is the height of this column, a fire broke out in the dead of night, which, the wind blowing devoured even distant buildings,

and rushed devastating through every quarter with astonishing swiftness and noise. It consumed 89 churches, gates, the Guildhall, public edifices, hospitals, schools, libraries, a great number of blocks of buildings, 13,200 houses, 400 streets. Of the 26 Wards, it utterly destroyed 15, and left 8 mutilated and half-burnt. The ashes of the City, covering as many as 436 acres, extended on one side from the Tower along the bank of the Thames to the Church of the Templars, on the other side from the north-east gate along the walls to the head of Fleet-Ditch. Merciless to the wealth and estates of the citizens, it was harmless to their lives, so as throughout to remind us of the final destruction of the world by fire. The havoc was swift. A little space of time saw the same City most prosperous and no longer in being. On the third day, when it had now altogether vanquished all human counsel and resource, at the bidding, as we may well believe of heaven, the fatal fire stayed its course and everywhere died out.

(But popish frenzy, which wrought such horrors, is not yet quenched.)

These last words were added in 1631 and finally deleted in 1830.

From this holocaust good did arise and a "new", better proportioned, and healthier London was born. This was not before time since the bubonic plague, in 1665, had killed forty per cent of London's population.[2]

The King's proclamation of the tenth of September, required that all houses were, in the future, to be built of brick and stone and no longer of timber and thatch. In February 1667 new building laws came into force which, amongst other things, regulated the height, elevation and materials of new houses and required important streets to be at least sixty feet wide and alleys at least sixteen feet wide.[2]

SOURCE REFERENCES
1. Stuart London, Discovering London 5.
2. In Search of London.

The Monument.

PART 2

DICK WHITTINGTON'S CAT
THE FABLE

INTRODUCTION

After reading the facts of Dick Whittington's life, you may not believe that I existed or had anything to do with his rightful place in history, especially that of the City of London. However, as a cat, with a proud lineage, I am very pleased to be associated with such a man as Dick Whittington and even if I had been his "cat", I'm sure he would have treated me with the same care and regard that he showed to the poor and rich alike in his lifetime.

My popular association with Dick Whittington, has its beginnings in the very early custom and practice of ship-owning merchants to venture, together with their usual cargoes, the possessions of those known to them who were relatively poor, such as their apprentices.[1] A "venture" could encompass any item of trade, but in this context, it was a cat. A successful "venture" was one that was sold in a foreign country for a handsome profit.

The story of the venturing of a cat can be discovered from early times in many countries, both of southern and northern Europe. A Persian version is also known as early as the end of the thirteenth century. Furthermore, Ralston in his "Russian Folk-Tales" and Clouston in his "Popular Tales and Fictions, 1887", both suggest a Buddhistic origin for the story.

The English version of the story is unique in that an historical personage, namely Dick Whittington, was chosen as the central character.[1]

Naturally when we, cats, have been regarded by so many people in so many lands as bringers of good luck and fortune to those most in need and to those who have treated us with kindness, we have acquired our share of detractors.

These detractors basically launched a two-pronged attack on our very existence.

Firstly, since the French language was extensively spoken by the educated English in medieval times, and since trading for profit was known as "achat", our detractors anglicised "achat" into "a cat".[1]

Secondly, it was suggested, quite wrongly, that Dick Whittington, the merchant, was very much involved in the import and export of coal. Since a three-masted Norwegian vessel, much used in the coal trade, was called a "cat", this fact was used to explain away my very existence.[2] As a cat with a proud heritage, I find this particular attack most offensive as the strong English prejudice against coal did not abate until Dick Whittington had been dead for some one hundred and fifty years, and also the vessels built in his lifetime were called "keels" or "hoys" and the crew "keelers".[2]

So I now invite you to read on and maybe leave you with a slight mental puzzle, namely, how much of me is fable and how much is fact?

Meeow!

SOURCE REFERENCES
1. Dictionary of National Biography.
2. Sir Richard Whittington.

EVIDENCE OF MY EXISTENCE?

IN SCULPTURE

Dick Whittington owned a house in Gloucester until 1460. During the repairs to this house in 1862 the stone floor of the cellar was dug up and there was revealed a figure of a boy carrying a cat.[1] Other sources have said that this piece of sculpture was a representation of "a small boy, not a sturdy youth, who was carrying a nondescript small animal". Also there seems to be some serious doubt and a lack of satisfactory evidence to attribute this sculpture to the work of a fifteenth century craftsman.[2]

As has been said earlier, Dick Whittington's executors rebuilt Newgate gaol with money he left. It is said that the executors commemorated the fable of Dick Whittington and his cat by representing a life-sized figure of Liberty, with a cat at his feet, in one of the niches on the west side of the gate. The belief that the cat carved on the front of the prison when it was rebuilt after the Great Fire of 1666 had existed on the repair to the prison by Dick Whittington's executors is not true.[2]

A sculpture of a boy and a cat could have been found in the Guildhall Museum until about 1982 and is quite definitely of fifteenth century origin.[1] This sculpture together with all the other items in the Guildhall Museum were subsequently transferred to the London Museum.

IN STAINED GLASS

A stained glass window in the south wall of St. Michael Paternoster Royal depicts Dick Whittington with a black cat at his heels. The cat is not of the kind, or breed, that we would recognise today, since amongst other things, the legs are much longer and in general proportions would resemble more a present-day dog.

Dick Whittington window in the Church of St. Michael Paternoster Royal.

IN PORTRAIT

In the first impression of an engraving by Renold Elstrack, Dick Whittington's right hand is shown resting upon a human skull. However, popular taste of the time, about 1590, forced the artist to replace the skull with a cat. This shows that the fable of Dick Whittington's cat was 'well-known at the time.[1]

Malcolm mentions a small portrait in the Mercers' Hall which has long since disappeared. The subject of this portrait was a man of about sixty years old, "in a fur-livery gown and a black cap such as the Yeomen of the Guard now wear" and with a black and white cat on the left-hand side. The inscription on the portrait "R. Whittington, 1536", suggests that it was an adaptation of a portrait of Robert Whittington, the grammarian who lived from about 1480 to 1520, and not the supposed likeness of Dick Whittington.[3] The present portrait of Dick Whittington in the Mercers' Hall is relatively modern (1784 or earlier) and is engraved in Thornton's, "New History, Description and Survey of London".[2]

An illumination at the beginning of the ordinances for the Whittington Almshouse shows him on his deathbed surrounded by his executors and bedesmen.[2]

IN THE FLESH

As has already been mentioned, the blitz on London in 1940, which devastated the church and Whittington's tomb, also brought to light a very well preserved, and almost mummified, body of a cat. This cat had the typical long legs of Dick Whittington's time, but was of a general brown colour. There was no doubt in the minds of those workmen who had been sent to repair the church that the cat had been originally in the same tomb as the remains of Dick Whittington. It must be assumed that the cat had been placed in Dick Whittington's tomb after he was reinterred following the Great Fire of 1666, but the reason for, and the purpose behind, such an action is not known.

SOURCE REFERENCES
1. Sir Richard Whittington.
2. Dictionary of National Biography.
3. Londinium Redivivum.

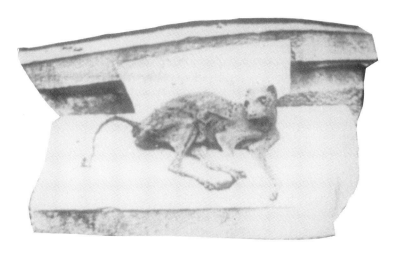

Body of the Cat found in Dick Whittington's tomb.

THE FABLE (ENGLISH VERSION)

The fable is very elegantly described in the Dictionary of National Biography in the following words:—

"Starting life as a poor ill-treated orphan in the west of England, he made his way to London on hearing that its streets were paved with gold. Arriving in a state of destitution he attracted the commiseration of a rich merchant, one Mr. Hugh Fitzwarren, who placed him as a scullion in his kitchen, where he suffered greatly from the tyranny of the cook, tempered only by the kindness of his master's daughter, Mrs. Alice. From this state of misery he was presently released by a strange piece of good fortune. It was the worthy merchant's custom when sending out a ship to let each of his servants venture something in it, in order that God might give him a greater blessing. To the freight of the good ship Unicorn, Dick Whittington could only contribute his cat, which he had bought for a penny to keep down the vermin in his garret; but the vessel happening to touch at an unknown part of the Barbary coast, the King of the country, whose palace was overrun with rats and mice, bought the cat for ten times more than all the freight besides.

"Meanwhile, Dick, unconscious of his good luck and driven desperate by the cook's ill usage, stole away from Leadenhall Street early in the morning of All Hallows Day, and left the City behind him, but as he rested at Holloway he heard Bow Bells ring out a merry peal which seemed to say:

'Turn again, Whittington, Lord Mayor of London.'

"Whereupon he returned to his pots and spits and, the

Unicorn soon coming in, married Mrs. Alice and rose to be thrice Lord Mayor of London and entertained Henry V, after his conquest of France, at a great feast, in the course of which he threw into the fire the King's bonds of thirty-seven thousand marks."[1]

Samuel Lysons provided a variation to the fable, saying:

"That the Mercer gave the domestics the chance of bettering their condition by having shares in fitting out ships to trade on the coast of the Barbary (Guinea). Richard had nothing to offer. A malicious fellow apprentice was envious of Richard's steadiness of character and jealous of the pleasure he enjoyed caressing the kitten which he had bought for a penny, suggesting that Richard must venture his cat. The cat became the favourite of the ship and on arrival customary bartering with a barbarous nation took place. The King invited the Captain to dinner but swarms of rats ran over the table and carried off the meat. The Captain suggested the cat was the remedy and was invited to dinner the next day. The cat was released and cleared the rats. The King and Queen offered to give a rich casket of jewels for so valuable an animal. The Captain reported the success on his return home and the honest merchant handed it all over to Richard to the disgust of the apprentice who had suggested the cat."

When, according to Samuel Lysons, Dick Whittington left London, depressed, he sat down at a milestone and then heard Bow Bells. He further states that the stone commemorating the spot was in fact the base plinth of an ancient village cross at the foot of Highgate Hill.[2] This original stone cross of St. Anthony, where alms and charitable gifts were left, was replaced in 1735 by the first Whittington Stone.[3]

The "legend" of Dick Whittington is not known to have been narrated prior to 1605.[1]

SOURCE REFERENCES

1. Dictionary of National Biography.
2. The Model Merchant of the Middle Ages.
3. The Hospital on the Hill.

PUBLIC PERFORMANCES

On the eighth of February 1604, or 1605, a dramatic version of the fable entitled, "The History of Richard Whittington of his lowe byrth, his great fortune, as yt was plaied by the prynces servants", was licensed for the press.[2]

On the sixteenth of July 1605 a licence was granted for the publication of a ballad called "The vertuous lyfe and memorable Death of Sir Richard Whittington, mercer, sometyme Lord Maiour".

Neither the above mentioned play or the ballad are known to have survived.[1]

The earliest form of the story, in the British Museum collection, is a black-letter ballad of 1641, entitled "London's glory and Whittington's renown; or a looking glass for the citizens of London; being a remarkable story of how Sir Richard Whittington . . . came to be three times Lord Mayor of London, and how his rise was by a cat".[1]

Finally, and to bring the fable into all our present day lives, the pantomime performance of Christmas 1985, given by the Players' Theatre in London's Villiers Street, must be mentioned. The pantomime was called, "Whittington Junior and his Sensation Cat", by H. J. Byron (1862) and this adaptation also combined, "Dick Whittington" by Robert Reece (1870). It was a truly memorable experience, most excellently adapted and performed by all and a fitting denouement to the fable of Dick Whittington and his Cat. The Players' Theatre do their own adaptations but, in this instance, the originals can be found in the British Museum.

SOURCE REFERENCES
1. Dictionary of National Biography.
2. Stationers' Registers.

BIBLIOGRAPHY

The Model Merchant of the Middle Ages—(London 1860) by Samuel Lysons.

Survey of London—by J. Stow (Edited by Strype).

Medieval London—Discovering London 3—by Kenneth Derwent (First published in 1968 by MacDonald & Co. Ltd.).

History of England—by William McElwee: *Teach Yourself Books*—(First published in 1960 by the English Universities Press Ltd.).

Sir Richard Whittington—(1881) by W. Besant and J. Rice.

Memorials of London and London Life in the XIIIth, XIVth and XVth Centuries—extracts from the Early Archives of the City of London A.D. 1276-1419. Translated and Edited by Henry Thomas Riley.

Reign of Henry V—by J. H. Wylie.

Dictionary of National Biography, volume 21—Edited by Sir Leslie Stephen and Sir Sydney Lee.

Old English Customs and Ceremonies—by F. J. Drake-Carnell (First published in 1938 by B. T. Batsford Ltd., London).

Tudor London—Discovering London 4—by A. G. Robertston (First published in 1968 by MacDonald & Co. Ltd.).

Encyclopedia Britannica.

Life in Medieval England—by J. J. Bagley (First published in 1960 by B. T. Batsford Ltd., London).

Letts Visit London—by Frederick Tingey (First published in 1977 by Charles Letts & Co. Ltd., London).

In Search of London—by H. V. Morton (First published in 1951 by Methuen & Co. Ltd., London).

St. Michael Paternoster Royal—church pamphlet.

They Saw It Happen, 55 B.C.-1485—compiled by W. O. Hassall (First published in 1957 by Basil Blackwell, Oxford).

Stuart London—Discovering London 5—by Malpas Pearse (First published in 1969 by MacDonald & Co. Ltd).

*History of Dorset—3rd Edition by Hutchins.

*History of Henry IV—by J. H. Wylie

*Ordinances of the Privy Council—ed. Nicholas.

*Annales Ricardi II—Rolls Series.

*Monasticon Anglicanum—ed. Caley, Ellis and Bandinel.

*MS. Galba, B5—by Cotton.

*Foedera—Original ed. by Rymer.

*Issue of the Exchequer—by Devon.

*Londinium Redivivum—by Malcolm.

*Stationers' Registers—by Arber.

The Mercers' Company of the City of London and its Hall—A Mercers' Company publication.

Execution Bell—Church of the Holy Sepulchre, London photographic publication.

A Short History of Fishmongers' Hall—A Fishmongers' Company publication.

Notes on Richard Whittington—A Mercers' Company publication.

The Merchant Class of Medieval London, 1300-1500—by Sylvia L. Thrupp (First published in 1962 as an Ann Arbor paperback by The University of Michigan Press).

The Charity of Richard Whittington—by Jean Imray (First published in 1968 by the University of London, The Athlone Press).

Guildhall Records Office—Viewers' Reports.

Historical collections of a citizen of London in the 15th century—edited by James Gairdner, Camden Society 1876.

The History of St. Bartholomew's Hospital—by Norman Moore, M.D. (Published in 1918 by C. Arthur Pearson Ltd.).

Guildhall Records Office—Husting Roll.

Calendar to the Patent Rolls, Henry IV 1408-1413.

Calendar of Letter Book I of the City of London, Henry IV and V—edited by R. Sharpe 1909.

St. Bartholomew's Hospital Records—Cartulary of John Cok.

Charities of London—by Jordan.

Calendar to the Patent Rolls, Richard III, 1391-6.

Mercers' Company—Wardens' Accounts.

Public Records Office—Chancery Inquisitions Post Mortem.

Register of Henry Chichele.

Public Records Office—Early Chancery Proceedings and Chancery Extent for Debt.

Calendar of Records of the Skinners' Company, January 1965.

Old and New London—(Published by Cassell, Petter and Galpin).

The Church of Saint Giles, Coberley—church pamphlet.

St. John The Evangelist, Pauntley—church pamphlet.

Mercers' Company—Acts of Court.

Calendar of Plea and Memoranda Rolls.

The Hospital on the Hill—(First published in 1985 by the Whittington Hospital History Project).

Gloucester Cathedral—publication by the Very Rev. Seiriol Evans and revised by the Very Rev. Gilbert Thurlow.

* Extracts from *Dictionary of National Biography, Vol. 21.*

R H   MAR 2. 0 0. 3